UNDERSTANDING THE SERMON ON MOUNT

A Commentary on the Sermon on the Mount using Ancient Bible Study Methods

Michael Harvey Koplitz

This edition 2018 copyright © by Michael H. Koplitz
All rights reserved. No part of this publication may be reproduced or transmitted in any form or by any means without permission of the publisher.

All Scripture quotations, unless otherwise noted, are taken from the New American Standard Bible®, Copyright © 1960, 1962, 1963, 1968, 1971, 1972, 1973, 1975, 1977, 1995 by the Lockman Foundation. Used by permission. (www.Lockman.org)

The NASB uses italic to indicate words that have been added for clarification. Citations are shown with large capital letters.

Published by Michael H. Koplitz

Table of Contents

ACKNOWLEDGMENTS

This work could not have been accomplished without Dr. Anne Davis, who taught me Ancient (Hebraic) Bible study methods, and my two study partners, Rev. Dr. Robert Cook and Pastor Sandra Koplitz. We know that the journey has just started and will last a lifetime. The discovery of the depths of God's Word is waiting for us to find.

Introduction

While I was attending Seminary earning my M. Div. degree, I started to question what the instructors and reference books were saying about the Scriptures. One of the ideas being offered then was that the Bible was full of errors and not factual. I found that attitude disturbing for Seminary instructors to be teaching. After all, the Seminary experience is to train pastors to go out into God's world and preach the Bible. How can you preach the Bible if you believe what these instructors are teaching? The methods that were being taught to examine the Bible just seemed inaccurate to me.

After graduating from Seminary, I spent a lot of time reading different views about the Bible. I eventually read the Zohar. This collection of midrashim is considered the secret work of the Torah, according to Kabbalists. In addition, I read quite a bit about Messianic Judaism. Their view of the Bible is quite different than the Seminary view.

I decided that the biblical interpretation that was being taught in Seminary was not the biblical interpretation the people heard when Jesus Christ (whose Hebraic name is Yeshua) preached. I went on a quest to learn what the people of Yeshua's day thought about Scripture, and what they thought when the Scriptures were read. This quest led me to Dr. Anne Davis and The Bible Learning University. Dr. Davis was in search of the same thing I was searching. She had made many discoveries that helped me in my quest. I earned the Ph. D. degree from The Bible Learning University in Hebraic Studies in Christianity concentrating on ancient Bible Studies methods.

Finally, I found someone who believed that the church has placed almost 1900 years of their theological ideas about the Scriptures and in many places possibly distorting its original meaning. What is also important to hear is that the basic tenants of Yeshua as God's Messiah, my Lord and Savior are in the Bible. My faith in Yeshua is stronger now that I have learned from Dr. Davis how to study the Scriptures in the same manner that the people did in Yeshua's day.

I have included an article that describes the differences between Greek learning methods and Hebraic learning methods. Please do not skip this chapter unless you are familiar with ancient Bible study methods because if you do then the analysis and commentary that follows may become difficult for you to understand.

Our God is vast and infinite and so is His Word. May God bless you in your discovery of what God's Word is about.

This work is a commentary on Yeshua's Sermon on the Mount using Ancient Bible Study Methods. If you are unfamiliar with this method, you will want to read the next two chapters. You may want to visit http://bibleinteract.tv for lessons on Ancient Bible Study Methods.

The main differences between the Greek method and Hebraic method of teaching

Once you are aware of the two teaching styles, you will be able to determine if you are in a class or reading a book, whether the analysis and/or teaching method is either in a Greek or Hebraic method. In the Greek method, it is automatically thought that the instructor is right because of advanced knowledge. In the college situation, it is because the professor has his/her Ph.D. in some area of study, so one assumes that he or she knows everything about the topic. For example, Rodney Dangerfield played the role of a middle-aged man going to college. His English midterm was to write about Kurt Vonnegut Jr. Since he didn't understand any of Vonnegut's books he hired Vonnegut himself to the write the midterm. When it was returned to him, the English Professor told Dangerfield that whoever wrote the paper knew nothing about Vonnegut. This is an example of the Greek method of teaching. Did the Ph.D. English professor think that she knew more about Vonnegut's writings than Vonnegut did? [1]

In the Greek teaching method, the professor or the instructor claims to be the authority. If you are attending a Bible study class and the class leader says, "I will teach you the only way to understand this biblical book," you may want to consider the implications. This method is common since most Seminaries and Bible colleges teach a Greek method of learning, which is the same method the church has been utilizing for centuries.

---

[1] *Back to School*. Performed by Rodney Dangerfield. Hollywood: CA: Paper Clip Productions, 1986. DVD.

Hebraic teaching methods are different. The teacher wants the students to challenge what they hear. It is through questioning that a student can learn. In addition, the teacher wants his/her students to excel to a point where the student becomes the teacher.

It is said that if two rabbis come together to discuss a passage of Scripture, the result will be at least ten different opinions. All points of view are acceptable if the points can be supported by biblical evidence. It is permissible and encouraged for students to have multiple opinions. There is a depth to God's Word, and God wants us to find all His messages that are placed in the Scriptures.

Seeking out the meaning of the Scriptures beyond the literal meaning is essential to fully understanding God's Word.[2] The Greek method of learning the Scriptures has prevailed over the centuries. One problem is that only the literal interpretation of Scripture was often viewed as valid, as prompted by Martin Luther's "sola literalis" meaning that only the literal interpretation of Scripture was valid. The Fundamentalist movements of today are generally based on the literal interpretation of the Scripture. Therefore, they do not believe that God placed any deeper, hidden, or secret meanings in the Word.

The students of the Scriptures who learn through Hebraic training and understanding have drawn a different conclusion. The Hebrew language itself leads to different possible interpretations because of the construction of the language. The Hebraic method of Bible study opens avenues of thought about God's revelations in the Scripture that may have never been considered. A question may be raised about the Scripture being studied for which there may not be an immediate answer. If so, it becomes the responsibility of the learners

____

[2] Davis, Anne Kimball. *The Synoptic Gospels.* MP3. Albuquerque: NM: BibleInteract, 2012.

to uncover the meaning. Also, remember that multiple opinions about the meaning of Scripture are also acceptable if they can be supported by Scripture.

Methodology

The methodology employed is to use First Century Scripture study methods integrated with the customs and culture of Yeshua's day to examine the Hebrew and Christian Scriptures, thus gathering a deeper understanding by learning the Scriptures in the way the people of Yeshua's day did.

The Process of Discovery

I have titled the methodology of analyzing a passage of Scripture in a Hebraic manner the "Process of Discovery." This methodology was developed by the author bringing together the various areas of linguistic and cultural understanding. There are several sections to the process and not all the sections apply to every passage of Scripture. The overall result of developing this process is to give the reader a framework into the ideas being presented.

The "Process of Discovery" starts with a Scripture passage. If the passage is in a poetic form, it is identified. Possible poetic techniques include: parallelism, chiastic structures, and repetition. Formatting the passage in its poetic form allows the reader to be able to visualize what the first century CE listener was hearing. The chiasms are labeled by their corresponding sections, for example: A, B, C, B', A'. Not all passages of the Scriptures have a poetic form.

The next step is to "question the narrative," which is accomplished by assuming the reader knows nothing about the passage. Therefore, the questions go from the simple to the complex. The next task is to identify any linguistic patterns. Linguistic patterns include, but are not limited to: irony, simile, metaphor, symbolism, idioms, hyperbole, figurative language, personification, and allegory.

Any translation inconsistencies discovered between the English NASB version and either the Hebrew or Greek versions are identified. There are times when a Hebrew or Greek word can be translated in more than one way. Inconsistencies also can be created by the translation committee, which may have decided to use traditional language instead of the actual translation. The decision of the translation committee can be generally found in the Preface or Introduction to the Bible. Perhaps some of the inconsistencies were intentionally added to convey some deeper meaning therefore, the inconsistencies need to be examined.

Echoes of the Hebrew Scriptures in the Christian Scripture are identified. This occurs when a passage from the Hebrew Scripture is used in the Christian Scripture or when a command is directly discussed in the Christian Scriptures. [3] In addition, echoes can be found when Torah (Genesis through Deuteronomy) passages are used in other Hebrew Bible books. In addition to echoes, cross references are listed. A cross reference is a reference to another verse in the Scripture which can assist the reader to understand the verse that is being read.

The names of persons mentioned in the passage are listed. Many of the Hebrew names have meaning and may be associated with places or actions. Jewish parents used to name their children based on what they felt God had in store for their child. An example of this is Abraham whose original name was Abram and was changed to mean eternal father (in this case Abram's name was changed by God to Abraham indicating a function he was to perform). When the Hebrew Bible gives names, many of the occurrences will indicate something special to the reader/listener. The same importance can hold true for the names of places. The time it takes to travel between places can supply insight to the event.

---

[3] Mitzvot are the 613 commandments found in the Torah that please God. There are positive and negative commandments. The list was first development by Maimonides. The full list can be found at: ttp://www.jewfaq.org/613.htm.

Key phrases are identified in a verse when they are important to an understanding of that passage. There are no rules for selecting the key phrases. Searching for other occurrences of the phrase in Scripture can be done to understand how the phrase was being used; this must be done in either Hebrew or Greek, not in English. Examining phrases instead of singular words allows the words in question to be seen in their context.

The Rules of Hillel for Bible understanding can be used when applicable. Hillel was a Torah scholar who lived shortly before Yeshua's day. Hillel developed several rules for Torah students to interpret the Scriptures which are referred to as halachic midrash. In several cases these rules are helpful in the analysis of the Scripture.

After the linguistic analysis is complete an examination of the cultural implications will be examined. The culture is important because it is not specifically referenced in the biblical narratives as indicated earlier.

From the linguistic analysis and the cultural understanding, it is possible to obtain a deeper meaning of the Scripture beyond the literal meaning of the plain text. That is what the listeners of Yeshua's time were doing. They put the linguistics and the culture together without even having to contemplate it. They simply did it.

This will lead to a conclusion or a set of conclusions about what the passage is talking about. Most of the time the Hebraic analysis leads to the desire for a deeper analysis to fully understand what Yeshua was talking about or what was happening to Him. Whatever the result, a new deeper understanding of the Scripture will be obtained.

The components of the Process of Discovery are:

Language

Process of Discovery

    Linguistics Section

        Linguistic Structure

        Discussion

    Questioning the Passage

    Verse Comparison on citations or proof text

    Translation Inconsistencies

    Biblical Personalities

    Biblical Locations

    Phrase Study

    Scripture cross references

    Linguistic Echoes

    Rules of Hillel

Culture Section

Discussion

Questioning the passage

Cultural Echoes

Culture and Linguistics Section

Discussion

Midrash

Zohar

Thoughts

Reflections

(Only sections that are relevant to the passage are used)

Abbreviations

Bibleworks V10[4] was used for the Scriptures used in this study guide. Below are the abbreviations used in the software.

Pentateuch	GEN	EXO	LEV	NUM	DEU
Historical & Poetic	JOS 1KI NEH ECC	JDG 2KI EST SOL	RUT 1CH JOB	1SA 2CH PSA	2SA EZR PRO
Prophets	ISA HOS MIC ZEC	JER JOE NAH MAL	LAM AMO HAB	EZE OBA ZEP	DAN JON HAG
Gospels	MAT	MAR	LUK	JOH	ACT
Paul	ROM PHI 2TI	1CO COL TIT	2CO 1TH PHM	GAL 2TH	EPH 1TI
Apostles	HEB 2JO	JAM 3JO	1PE JUD	2PE REV	1JO
Apocrypha	1ES 3MA PSS PRA JDT 4MA	BAR PRM TOB ODE EPJ PSX	1MA WIS SUS 4ES 2MA SIP	SIR BEL LAO ESG JSA JDA	TBS SUT DAT BET DNG

The following is a list of aliases for BibleWorks book name abbreviations. See the <u>Book Names</u> section of the Options window for details on how to add to or change these aliases.

---

[4] "Bible Version Abbreviations." *Abbreviations*. N.p., n.d. Web. 29 Oct. 2016.

Internal Name	Name used in Browse Window	Name used in Exported Verse Lists	Alias 1	Alias 2
Gen	Genesis	Gen.	Gen	Genesis
Exo	Exodus	Exod.	Exo	Exodus
Lev	Leviticus	Lev.	Lev	Leviticus
Num	Numbers	Num.	Num	Numbers
Deu	Deuteronomy	Deut.	Deu	Deuteronomy
Jos	Joshua	Jos.	Jos	Joshua
Jdg.	Judges	Jdg.	Jdg	Judges
Rut	Ruth	Ruth	Rut	Ruth
1Sa	1 Samuel	1 Sam.	1Sa	1Samuel
2Sa	2 Samuel	2 Sam.	2Sa	2Samuel
1Ki	1 Kings	1 Ki.	1Ki	1Kings
2Ki	2 Kings	2 Ki.	2Ki	2Kings
1Ch	1 Chronicles	1 Chr.	1Ch	1Chronicles
2Ch	2 Chronicles	2 Chr.	2Ch	2 Chronicles
Ezr	Ezra	Ezr.	Ezr	Ezra
Neh	Nehemiah	Neh.	Neh	Nehemiah
Est	Esther	Est.	Est	Esther
Job	Job	Job	Job	Job
Psa	Psalm	Ps.	Psa	Psalm
Pro	Proverbs	Prov.	Pro	Proverbs
Ecc	Ecclesiastes	Eccl.	Ecc	Ecclesiastes
Sol	Song of Solomon	Cant.	Sol	Song
Isa	Isaiah	Isa.	Isa	Isaiah
Jer	Jeremiah	Jer.	Jer	Jeremiah
Lam	Lamentations	Lam.	Lam	Lamentations
Eze	Ezekiel	Ezek.	Eze	Ezekiel
Dan	Daniel	Dan.	Dan	Daniel
Hos	Hosea	Hos.	Hos	Hosea
Joe	Joel	Joel	Joe	Joel
Amo	Amos	Amos	Amo	Amos
Oba	Obadiah	Obad.	Oba	Obadiah

Jon	Jonah	Jon.	Jon	Jonah
Mic	Micah	Mic.	Mic	Micah
Nah	Nahum	Nah.	Nah	Nahum
Hab	Habakkuk	Hab.	Hab	Habakkuk
Zep	Zephaniah	Zeph.	Zep	Zephaniah
Hag	Haggai	Hag.	Hag	Haggai
Zec	Zechariah	Zech.	Zec	Zechariah
Mal	Malachi	Mal.	Mal	Malachi
Mat	Matthew	Matt.	Mat	Matthew
Mar	Mark	Mk.	Mar	Mark
Luk	Luke	Lk.	Luk	Luke
Joh	John	Jn.	Joh	John
Act	Acts	Acts	Act	Acts
Rom	Romans	Rom.	Rom	Romans
1Co	1 Corinthians	1 Co.	1Co	1Corinthians
2Co	2 Corinthians	2 Co.	2Co	2Corinthians
Gal	Galatians	Gal.	Gal	Galatians
Eph	Ephesians	Eph.	Eph	Ephesians
Phi	Philippians	Phil.	Phi	Philippians
Col	Colossians	Col.	Col	Colossians
1Th	1 Thessalonians	1 Thess.	1Th	1Thessalonians
2Th	2 Thessalonians	2 Thess.	2Th	2Thessalonians
1Ti	1 Timothy	1 Tim.	1Ti	1Timothy
2Ti	2 Timothy	2 Tim.	2Ti	2Timothy
Tit	Titus	Tit.	Tit	Titus
Phm	Philemon	Phlm.	Phm	Philemon
Heb	Hebrews	Heb.	Heb	Hebrews
Jam	James	Jas.	Jam	James
1Pe	1 Peter	1 Pet.	1Pe	1Peter
2Pe	2 Peter	2 Pet.	2Pe	2Peter
1Jo	1 John	1 Jn.	1Jo	1John
2Jo	2 John	2 Jn.	2Jo	2John
3Jo	3 John	3 Jn.	3Jo	3John
Jud	Jude	Jude	Jud	Jude

Rev	Revelation	Rev.	Rev	Revelation
1Es	1 Esdras	1 Es.	1Es	1Esdras
Jdt	Judith	Jdt.	Jdt	Judith
Tob	Tobit	Tob.	Tob	Tobit
1Ma	1 Maccabees	1 Ma.	1Ma	1Maccabees
2Ma	2 Maccabees	2 Ma.	2Ma	2Maccabees
3Ma	3 Maccabees	3 Ma.	3Ma	3Maccabees
4Ma	4 Maccabees	4 ma.	4Ma	4Maccabees
Ode	Odes	Odes	Ode	Odes
Wis	Wisdom	Wis.	Wis	Wisdom
Sir	Sirach	Sir.	Sir	Sirach
Sip	Sip	Sip	Sip	Sip
Pss	Psalms of Solomon	Ps. Sol.	Pss	
Bar	Baruch	Bar.	Bar	Baruch
Epj	Epistle of Jeremiah	Ep. Jer.	Epj	
Sus	Susanna	Sus.	Sus	Susanna
Bel	Bel	Bel.	Bel	Bel
Pra	Prayer of Azariah	Pr. Az.	Pra	Azariah
Dng	Daniel (Greek)	Dng	Dng	Dng
Prm	Prayer of Manasseh	Pr. Man.	Prm	Manasseh
Psx	Psalm(151)	Psx.	Psx	
Lao	Laodiceans	Lao.	Lao	Laodiceans
4Es	4 Esdras	4 Es.	4Es	4Esdras
Esg	Esther (Greek)	Esg.	Esg	
Jsa	Joshua (A)	Jsa.	Jsa	
Jda	Judges (A)	Jda.	Jda	
Tbs	Tobit (S)	Tbs.	Tbs	
Sut	Susanna (TH)	Sut.	Sut	
Dat	Daniel (TH)	Dat.	Dat	
Bet	Bel (TH)	Bet.	Bet	
WCF	WCF	WCF	WCF	
WLC	WLC	WLC	WLC	
WSC	WSC	WSC	WSC	

Matthew 5:1-11

Language

New American Standard 1995	Koine Greek
[1] When Jesus saw the crowds, He went up on the mountain; and after He sat down, His disciples came to Him. [2] He opened His mouth and *began* to teach them, saying, [3] "Blessed are the poor in spirit, for theirs is the kingdom of heaven. [4] "Blessed are those who mourn, for they shall be comforted. [5] "Blessed are the gentle, for they shall inherit the earth. [6] "Blessed are those who hunger and thirst for righteousness, for they shall be satisfied. [7] "Blessed are the merciful, for they shall receive mercy. [8] "Blessed are the pure in heart, for they shall see God. [9] "Blessed are the peacemakers, for they shall be called sons of God. [10] "Blessed are those who have been persecuted for the sake of righteousness, for theirs is the kingdom of heaven. [11] "Blessed are you when *people* insult you and persecute you, and falsely say all kinds of evil against you because of Me.	[1] Ἰδὼν δὲ τοὺς ὄχλους ἀνέβη εἰς τὸ ὄρος, καὶ καθίσαντος αὐτοῦ προσῆλθαν αὐτῷ οἱ μαθηταὶ αὐτοῦ· [2] καὶ ἀνοίξας τὸ στόμα αὐτοῦ ἐδίδασκεν αὐτοὺς λέγων· [3] Μακάριοι οἱ πτωχοὶ τῷ πνεύματι, ὅτι αὐτῶν ἐστιν ἡ βασιλεία τῶν οὐρανῶν. [4] μακάριοι οἱ πενθοῦντες, ὅτι αὐτοὶ παρακληθήσονται. [5] μακάριοι οἱ πραεῖς, ὅτι αὐτοὶ κληρονομήσουσιν τὴν γῆν. [6] μακάριοι οἱ πεινῶντες καὶ διψῶντες τὴν δικαιοσύνην, ὅτι αὐτοὶ χορτασθήσονται. [7] μακάριοι οἱ ἐλεήμονες, ὅτι αὐτοὶ ἐλεηθήσονται. [8] μακάριοι οἱ καθαροὶ τῇ καρδίᾳ, ὅτι αὐτοὶ τὸν θεὸν ὄψονται. [9] μακάριοι οἱ εἰρηνοποιοί, ὅτι αὐτοὶ υἱοὶ θεοῦ κληθήσονται. [10] μακάριοι οἱ δεδιωγμένοι ἕνεκεν δικαιοσύνης, ὅτι αὐτῶν ἐστιν ἡ βασιλεία τῶν οὐρανῶν. [11] μακάριοί ἐστε ὅταν ὀνειδίσωσιν ὑμᾶς καὶ διώξωσιν καὶ εἴπωσιν πᾶν πονηρὸν καθ᾽ ὑμῶν [ψευδόμενοι] ἕνεκεν ἐμοῦ. [12] χαίρετε καὶ ἀγαλλιᾶσθε, ὅτι ὁ μισθὸς ὑμῶν πολὺς ἐν τοῖς οὐρανοῖς· οὕτως γὰρ ἐδίωξαν τοὺς προφήτας τοὺς πρὸ ὑμῶν.

Process of Discovery

Linguistics Section

Linguistic Structure

[Transition][1] When Jesus saw the crowds, He went up on the mountain; and after He sat down, His disciples came to Him. [2] He opened His mouth and *began* to teach them, saying,

[Beattitudes] [3] "Blessed are the poor in spirit, for theirs is the kingdom of heaven.
[4] "Blessed are those who mourn, for they shall be comforted.
[5] "Blessed are the gentle, for they shall inherit the earth.
[6] "Blessed are those who hunger and thirst for righteousness, for they shall be satisfied.
[7] "Blessed are the merciful, for they shall receive mercy.
[8] "Blessed are the pure in heart, for they shall see God.
[9] "Blessed are the peacemakers, for they shall be called sons of God.
[10] "Blessed are those who have been persecuted for the sake of righteousness, for theirs is the kingdom of heaven.
[11] "Blessed are you when *people* insult you and persecute you, and falsely say all kinds of evil against you because of Me.

[12] "Rejoice and be glad, for your reward in heaven is great; for in the same way they persecuted the prophets who were before you.

Questioning the Passage[5]

1. Why did Yeshua go up a mountain to give this message? (v. 1)

   Matthew's Gospel seeks to Yeshua as the replacement for Moses. Moses was on

   Mount Sinai when he appeared before the people with the Ten Commandments.

---

[5] (The questions and answers offered are for discussion purposes. You may have different questions and answers. Remember all questions are valid and all answers must be defendable from Scripture.. This applies to this section and to the Culture Section.)

Culture Section

Discussion

Rocco Errico calls this section of Matthew's gospel "the Constitution of the kingdom of heaven." He said that Yeshua used four modes of communication with His followers:

1. Very terse language, short sayings that had a cutting-edge

2. He gave a vision of the kingdom of God in a new way by telling stories

3. He healed physical illnesses

4. He brought God to an outcast of society

The Beatitudes are Yeshua's understanding of truth and his interpretation of the Torah. Yeshua helped his disciples to practice the spirit of the Torah by helping them to see beyond the traditions of the elders and man-made rules and regulations.[6]

Questioning the passage

1. What does it mean that he opened his mouth in verse two?

This is an Aramaic Semitic idiom which means "to speak." It is not to be interpreted literally as describing an act of opening one's mouth.

Sometimes it can mean that the teacher has removed his hand from his mouth and was ready to speak and teach. So, what we are about to hear after Jesus opened his mouth was teachings.[7]

---

[6] Errico, Rocco A., and George M. Lamsa. "Chapter 5." *Aramaic Light on the Gospel of Matthew: A Commentary on the Teachings of Jesus from the Aramaic and Unchanged Near Eastern Customs*. Santa Fe, NM: Noohra Foundation, 2000. N. pag. Print.
[7] IBID.

Prelude to the Beatitudes: When we examine the Beatitudes, we need to be looking at what the culture and the language was at the time. Unfortunately, Matthew's Gospel was written in Koine Greek. If we look up the Greek words and the meanings behind them, we will probably miss a majority if not all the meaning behind each of the Beatitudes. Therefore, the culture will be examined but also, when appropriate, the corresponding Hebrew word will be examined for each of the Beatitudes so that we can get an understanding of what people thought when Yeshua was offering these items.

The first word of each Beatitudes is "blessed." The Koine Greek word used is Μακάριοι (makarioi), which means "happy." Christianity over the centuries adjusted the meaning of this word from happy to blessed. However, the culture in Yeshua's day was that only God can be blessed.

בָּרַךְ *barak* **Meaning:** *to kneel, bless,* is the Hebrew word which is used for "bless."

The following are some examples of where this word is used in the Scripture.

[NAU] **Genesis 1:22** God **blessed** them, saying, "Be fruitful and multiply, and fill the waters in the seas, and let birds multiply on the earth."

[NAU] **Genesis 1:28** God **blessed** them; and God said to them, "Be fruitful and multiply, and fill the earth, and subdue it; and rule over the fish of the sea and over the birds of the sky and over every living thing that moves on the earth."

[NAU] **Genesis 2:3** Then God **blessed** the seventh day and sanctified it, because in it He rested from all His work which God had created and made.

[NAU] **Genesis 5:2** He created them male and female, and He **blessed** them and named them Man in the day when they were created. (Gen. 5:2 NAU)

There are numerous passages in the Hebrew Scriptures that use this word. Almost every time the word bless or blessed is written it refers to God. The beginning of Hebrew prayers starts with the words "blessed are you Lord our God King of the universe." This indicates that to be blessed is a divine action and God is the only divine.

Therefore, in Yeshua's day he would not have blessed the people because the culture which developed from the Torah says that only God is blessed. The translation of Μακάριοι as "happy" is in line with the culture and language of Yeshua's day. Today we would say that Μακάριοι means "blessed." Another example of word change of usage by the church is in conjunction with Paul's usage of the word "agape," which originally meant love and over the centuries has become Christian love.

To understand what this first word of the Beatitudes should be, which is "happy," we need to look at the Hebrew word and concept for happy. In fact, in Beatitudes that were written by the Sages they always start with the word happy.

אֶשֶׁר *osher* **Meaning:** *happiness,* is the Hebrew word for happy or happiness. The following are a few examples where it is used in Hebrew Scriptures.

NAU **Genesis 30:13** Then Leah said, **"Happy** am I! For women will call me **happy."** So she named him Ashe (Gen. 30:13 NAU)

NAU **2 Chronicles 7:10** Then on the twenty-third day of the seventh month he sent the people to their tents, rejoicing and **happy** of heart because of the goodness that the LORD had shown to David and to Solomon and to His people Israel. (2 Chr. 7:10 NAU)

^{NAU} **Job 5:17** "Behold, how **happy** is the man whom God reproves, So do not despise the discipline of the Almighty.

^{NAU} **Jonah 4:6** So the LORD God appointed a plant and it grew up over Jonah to be a shade over his head to deliver him from his discomfort. And Jonah was extremely **happy** about the plant. (Jon. 4:6 NAU)

Except in the book of Ecclesiastes the Hebrew word אֲשֶׁר is translated as happy however, note that the happiness is caused by the Lord. Bringing forward this concept into the Beatitudes is that we are happy because of something God is going to do or did for us. In discussing each of the Beatitudes the word happy will be used instead of blessed. Since the new American Standard Bible uses the word "blessed, the Scripture will be displayed in that manner.

"Blessed are the poor in spirit, for theirs is the kingdom of heaven.

In the culture of the Middle East in Yeshua's day a person may be poor and uncultured, yet they could highly respected and honored because of their ancestry. Therefore, descendants of the line of King David who may be poor were still respected because of their lineage. There was also an attitude that some people would rather starve than to do manual labor because their ancestors were never employed in that type of work.

In Judaism during the last two centuries before the birth of Yeshua the term "poor" was a synonym for "pious" or "saintly."

Therefore, the beatitude could be rewritten using the culture of the day to read for us today as:

Happy are the pious in spirit for theirs is the kingdom of heaven.

"Blessed are those who mourn, for they shall be comforted.

Mourning was very common in Yeshua's day because there were constant revolutions and uprisings in the land and because the Romans were frequently persecuting the people. To show that the people were in constant morning women would cut their hair, heads would be bowed down, and they would be dressed in black. For the men they would have had their heads covered with black cloth and their faces would be expressing deep sorrow.

The Galilee area was a center for insurrection and that is why the Romans placed a legion of soldiers there. Galileans were very warlike people therefore, a lot of killing happened there.

What Yeshua was saying was that in the new kingdom in God's presence the mourners would be comforted and that their sorrow would be changed to joy because the oppressors, the Romans, would be no more.

Therefore, the beatitude could be rewritten using the culture of the day to read for us today as:

Happy are the people being oppressed because there will be no more oppression.

"Blessed are the gentle, for they shall inherit the earth.

Many of the English versions of the Bible use the word "meek" instead of "gentle." Semitic people had a proverb from that day which read: "the meek shall inherit the earth." It refers to a person who does not retaliate when some wrong is done against them. The meek or gentle person are those who practice nonresistance and submit to injustice even at great inconvenience. The meek and gentle person does not reward evil for evil. Meekness is a sword of the Spirit that destroys hatred thereby removing fear and enmity.

A rewrite of this beatitude will take several more words because of inherit cultural concepts and language.

Therefore, the beatitude could be rewritten using the culture of the day to read for us today as:

> Happy are those who do not retaliate against evil for they shall inherit the earth because evil will not be allowed in the kingdom of God

"Blessed are those who hunger and thirst for righteousness, for they shall be satisfied.

The hunger and thirst for righteousness is a cultural hunger and thirst for justice. This desire for the ethical justice based on the laws of the Torah. In Yeshua's time exploitation of the poor and injustice prevailed everywhere. When the Roman government officials or even the local officials levied heavy taxes upon the people, the people began to hunger for true justice. A way to console themselves during these harsh times was that they would dream of kind and honest rulers and officials who would take the place of their harsh leaders.

The concept of justice is the foundation of all world religions and democratic institutions. We need to understand that justice is another name for truth and the truth of God's law is justice based on the laws of the Torah. Yeshua was telling those who are thirsting for justice that one day it would come.

Therefore, the beatitude could be rewritten using the culture of the day to read for us today as:

> Happy are those who seek justice because justice will prevail in the kingdom of God

"Blessed are the merciful, for they shall receive mercy.

In this beatitude the merciful can also be called the compassionate. To be merciful and compassionate meant to be kind and charitable. It also meant that one would open one's doors to strangers and allow them into the house. Therefore, Yeshua is telling us that being kind and compassionate to strangers is of a divine nature. The concept of giving and receiving is in nature. Spiritually God gives to us and then God expects us to give it away. When we do this, we are completing a spiritual cycle. God offers compassion to those of us who give part or all of what God gives us away to help others.

Therefore, the beatitude could be rewritten using the culture of the day to read for us today as:

> Happy are those who are compassionate to others for God will show compassion to them.

"Blessed are the pure in heart, for they shall see God.

"Pure in heart" is an Aramaic idiom. It is referring to a sincere individual. It also could mean a person with a clear mind. It is a person who has a clear heart, as sinless as is humanly possible, which allows the mind to perceive the spiritual forces from God. It is difficult if not impossible to sense and feel God when one is full of emotions and definitely not possible of one has sin. All our actions whether they be good or bad, are formulated in our mind. It is believed that when the mind is cleared that we are reflecting the goodness of God and that we can then sense God's presence. These people are also the innocent men and women who would never think of harming other people. They can feel God's presence with them always and they know that God is good.

Therefore, the beatitude could be rewritten using the culture of the day to read for us today as:

> Happy are those who would never think of hurting others, thus they can see and feel God's presence with them.

"Blessed are the peacemakers, for they shall be called sons of God.

This beatitude needs to be understood in the respect of how people greeted each other in Yeshua's day. The term peace in Aramaic also means to surrender. Therefore, in the ancient near East when one person greeted another with the Aramaic word *shlama,* which in Hebrew would be shalom, it carried the idea of "I surrender to you." It also would have been understood as "be at peace." That is why the English translation today uses the word peacemakers. If you surrender to another person both of you would find peace. When you find yourself at peace you're able to open yourself up to the LORD and trust in him alone.

There were people that sat at the city gates who were acting as judges and would reconcile people's grievances who were called peacemakers. Until the previous century the Middle East did not have many government appointed judges. However, there were always the peacemakers who were trying to bring about reconciliation. Since judges and peacemakers did not get paid they acted with purity because they couldn't be bribed.

Yeshua told us that we need to settle things with our adversaries and make peace if we intend to be the children of God. Anger and hatred are not allowed in the kingdom of God.

Therefore, the beatitude could be rewritten using the culture of the day to read for us today as:

> Happy are those who settle conflict between people with fairness and justice, for they will be called children of God.

"Blessed are those who have been persecuted for the sake of righteousness, for theirs is the kingdom of heaven.

Yeshua knew that his interpretation of the Torah laws was going to cause problems inside of Judaism. He knew that those who followed him would be persecuted by the religious leadership that wanted to hold onto power more than they were concerned about truly interpreting the Torah properly. Yeshua's view of the kingdom of God all people, men, women, and children would be equal citizens. Participants in the new kingdom would share God's light thus, racial and class barriers would be eliminating, and national boundaries obliterated. People would care about each other, pray for each other, and be there for each other. Love would be the rule of the day. Only those who continued to follow Yeshua, thus were the righteous, would be allowed to enter the kingdom of God regardless of the persecution that would come upon them.

A rewrite of this beatitude will take several more words because of inherit cultural concepts and language.

Therefore, the beatitude could be rewritten using the culture of the day to read for us today as:

> Happy are those who follow the ways of Yeshua the Messiah no matter what anyone says to them which may be in contradiction to Yeshua's way for entry into God's kingdom is through discipleship to Yeshua.

"Blessed are you when *people* insult you and persecute you, and falsely say all kinds of evil against you because of Me.

This beatitude is a repetition of the previous one. Repetition is used in the ancient world to emphasize an important point. Following the ways of Yeshua, trying to be like him, trying to act like him, is the way into heaven. When one comes to discipleship with Yeshua there will be people around them that will insult them for believing in God especially in this manner. The true disciple will accept this insult as a badge of discipleship to Yeshua.

Therefore, the beatitude could be rewritten using the culture of the day to read for us today as:

> Happy are those whose discipleship to Yeshua stands up against all opposition, no matter what the forces of evil say about them or about Yeshua.

Matthew 5:13-20

Language

New American Standard 1995	Koine Greek
[13] "You are the salt of the earth; but if the salt has become tasteless, how can it be made salty *again*? It is no longer good for anything, except to be thrown out and trampled underfoot by men. [14] "You are the light of the world. A city set on a hill cannot be hidden; [15] nor does *anyone* light a lamp and put it under a basket, but on the lampstand, and it gives light to all who are in the house. [16] "Let your light shine before men in such a way that they may see your good works, and glorify your Father who is in heaven. [17] "Do not think that I came to abolish the Law or the Prophets; I did not come to abolish but to fulfill. [18] "For truly I say to you, until heaven and earth pass away, not the smallest letter or stroke shall pass from the Law until all is accomplished. [19] "Whoever then annuls one of the least of these commandments, and teaches others *to do* the same, shall be called least in the kingdom of heaven; but whoever keeps and teaches *them*, he shall be called great in the kingdom of heaven.	[13] Ὑμεῖς ἐστε τὸ ἅλας τῆς γῆς· ἐὰν δὲ τὸ ἅλας μωρανθῇ, ἐν τίνι ἁλισθήσεται; Εἰς οὐδὲν ἰσχύει ἔτι, εἰ μὴ βληθῆναι ἔξω καὶ καταπατεῖσθαι ὑπὸ τῶν ἀνθρώπων. [14] Ὑμεῖς ἐστε τὸ φῶς τοῦ κόσμου· οὐ δύναται πόλις κρυβῆναι ἐπάνω ὄρους κειμένη· [15] οὐδὲ καίουσιν λύχνον καὶ τιθέασιν αὐτὸν ὑπὸ τὸν μόδιον, ἀλλ᾽ ἐπὶ τὴν λυχνίαν, καὶ λάμπει πᾶσιν τοῖς ἐν τῇ οἰκίᾳ. [16] Οὕτως λαμψάτω τὸ φῶς ὑμῶν ἔμπροσθεν τῶν ἀνθρώπων, ὅπως ἴδωσιν ὑμῶν τὰ καλὰ ἔργα, καὶ δοξάσωσιν τὸν πατέρα ὑμῶν τὸν ἐν τοῖς οὐρανοῖς. [17] Μὴ νομίσητε ὅτι ἦλθον καταλῦσαι τὸν νόμον ἢ τοὺς προφήτας· οὐκ ἦλθον καταλῦσαι ἀλλὰ πληρῶσαι. [18] Ἀμὴν γὰρ λέγω ὑμῖν, ἕως ἂν παρέλθῃ ὁ οὐρανὸς καὶ ἡ γῆ, ἰῶτα ἓν ἢ μία κεραία οὐ μὴ παρέλθῃ ἀπὸ τοῦ νόμου, ἕως ἂν πάντα γένηται. [19] Ὃς ἐὰν οὖν λύσῃ μίαν τῶν ἐντολῶν τούτων τῶν ἐλαχίστων, καὶ διδάξῃ οὕτως τοὺς ἀνθρώπους, ἐλάχιστος κληθήσεται ἐν τῇ βασιλείᾳ τῶν οὐρανῶν· ὃς δ᾽ ἂν ποιήσῃ καὶ διδάξῃ, οὗτος μέγας κληθήσεται ἐν τῇ βασιλείᾳ τῶν οὐρανῶν. [20] Λέγω γὰρ ὑμῖν ὅτι ἐὰν μὴ περισσεύσῃ ἡ δικαιοσύνη ὑμῶν πλεῖον τῶν γραμματέων καὶ

[20] "For I say to you that unless your righteousness surpasses *that* of the scribes and Pharisees, you will not enter the kingdom of heaven.	Φαρισαίων, οὐ μὴ εἰσέλθητε εἰς τὴν βασιλείαν τῶν οὐρανῶν.

Process of Discovery

Linguistics Section

Linguistic Structure

A [13] "You are the salt of the earth;

    B but if the salt has become tasteless, how can it be made salty *again*?

        C It is no longer good for anything, except to be thrown out and trampled under foot by men.

A' [14] "You are the light of the world.

    B' A city set on a hill cannot be hidden; [15] nor does *anyone* light a lamp and put it under a basket, but on the lampstand, and it gives light to all who are in the house.

        C' [16] "Let your light shine before men in such a way that they may see your good works, and glorify your Father who is in heaven.

[A: Who are you? B: Parable C: Responses of other people][8]

A [17] "Do not think that I came to abolish the Law or the Prophets; I did not come to abolish but to fulfill.

B [18] "For truly I say to you, until heaven and earth pass away, not the smallest letter or stroke shall pass from the Law until all is accomplished.

A' [9] "Whoever then annuls one of the least of these commandments, and teaches others *to do* the same, shall be called least in the kingdom of heaven; but whoever keeps and teaches *them*, he shall be called great in the kingdom of heaven.

---

[8] " Literary Structure (chiasm, Chiasmus) of Gospel of Matthew." Literary Structure (chiasm, Chiasmus) of Each Pericopes of Gospel of Matthew. N.p., n.d. Web. 31 Jan. 2017.
http://www.bible.literarystructure.info/bible/40_Matthew_pericope_e.html#11.

B' [20] "For I say to you that unless your righteousness surpasses *that* of the scribes and Pharisees, you will not enter the kingdom of heaven.

[A: The Law and Commandments. B: Heaven][9]

Discussion

This passage of the Sermon on the Mount consists of two small chiasms. The first chiasm deals with us as disciples of Yeshua. The second chiasm deals with the purpose of Yeshua.

Questioning the Passage

1. Is doing good works a way to glorify God? (v. 16)

   Simple answer is "yes." The Zohar tells us that God will judge what good we did on judgment day. If Yeshua covers our sins, then what would we be judged upon? Our good works, the mitzvot we follow.

2. What does it mean that Yeshua came to fulfill the Law and the Prophets? (v. 17)

   Man-made interpretations that are created to obscure or destroy the law by creating false doctrines will not succeed because the power of God's law will not allow that to happen. Many of the man-made interpretations in Yeshua's day were intended to circumvent the law so that the religious ruling class could exert control upon the people.

   Yeshua was seen as a founder of the new religion by the religious elite and leadership therefore, they did all that they could in an effort to stop him. In those days, founders of new religions condemned the principles and practices of the established faith. Therefore, by Yeshua saying that he had come to fulfill the law, he was not

---

[9] IBID.

trying to establish a new religion. When the church decided to become a new religion, it suffered criticism from the old religious systems that were attempting to resist the growth of the new religion for they could lose followers.

Yeshua was a new prophet and his teachings did deviate from the religious leaders of his day. To stop Yeshua the religious leaders of the day were spreading false rumors that Yeshua's teachings were aimed against the Torah and against the prophets. Therefore, Yeshua told them that he came to fulfill the Torah and the prophets not to destroy them. Men at the synagogues, who had difficulty understanding Yeshua's message, would have said that Yeshua came to destroy Judaism by weakening the Torah and the prophets.

Yeshua advocated the enactment of the law and the prophets as God intended the Law and the prophets to be enacted.[10]

3. What needs to be accomplished? (v. 18)

   What needs to be accomplished is that the Torah is to be observed by all people on the Earth. The smallest letter refers to the Hebrew letter *yod* which is the smallest letter of the Hebrew alphabet. This letter also represents God. Since God will always exist whether the Law is obeyed or not, the letter *yod* Will exist reminding us that God wants the best for us.

4. What does it mean to be called "great" in Heaven? (v. 19)

---

[10] Errico, Rocco A., and George M. Lamsa. "Chapter 5." *Aramaic Light on the Gospel of Matthew: A Commentary on the Teachings of Jesus from the Aramaic and Unchanged Near Eastern Customs*. Santa Fe, NM: Noohra Foundation, 2000. N. pag. Print.

To be called great in heaven means that one is following all the commandments of the Torah.

5. What does it mean to surpass the righteousness of the scribes and Pharisees? (v. 20) Many of the Pharisees and Sadducees of Yeshua's day read, analyzed, and taught the Law but they did not live up to those principles. They showed their piety when they were in public and used long prayers so that people would think they were pious. But in their daily dealing with people they were far from what the Law said. Yeshua is telling us as His disciples that we are to go beyond the literal analysis of the Torah. Yeshua tells us that we need to practice and reveal the inner meaning of the Law. This methodology was new for this time. It was introduced via Hillel the Sage who lived before Yeshua. Questioning the Scripture and debating its meaning was relatively new.

The phrase "you will not enter the kingdom of heaven" means that unless you are practicing the principles of the kingdom you could not be a part of the kingdom of heaven. In the Aramaic version of verse 20 the word we translate as "enter" means "to participate." As followers of Yeshua we are to demonstrate the ways of the kingdom of heaven on earth.[11]

Scripture cross references

Verse 15	Mar 4:21; Luk 8:16; Luk 11:33; Phi 2:15
Verse 16	1 Pet 2:12

---

[11] IBID.

Culture Section

Discussion

"According to the <u>International Standard Bible Encyclopedia entry</u> on house construction, a roof was typically made of a straw and mud mixture. This would have consisted of timbers, covered with brush or similar thatching, and topped with mud and straw. This is apparently a wide-spread construction technique, and they also cite the use of a small roller that was used periodically after rain to smooth and compress the mud layer, making it progressively stronger."[12]

Unusable salt was thrown on the roof because it strengthened the roof. The salt would mix with the mud and straw which is already on the roof.

Questioning the passage

1. What is the symbolism of salt with respect to humans? (v. 13)

    Refer to question number two in the culture section.

2. What is the symbolism of the salt being trampled underfoot by men? (v. 13)

    From the beginning of time salt was considered a precious element. Salt became a currency, like gold and silver are today. The English word "Salary" is derived from the Latin word *sal* which means "salt." In Roman days soldiers and workers were paid in salt.

    There are two kinds of salt: sea salt and earth salt. Sea salt never loses its flavor. Earth mined salt must be kept dry or it loses its flavor. The chemistry must be that

---

12 "What Was the Roof Likely Made of in Mark 2:4?" History - What Was the Roof Likely Made of in Mark 2:4? - Biblical Hermeneutics Stack Exchange. N.p., n.d. Web. 01 Feb. 2017.
http://hermeneutics.stackexchange.com/questions/370/what-was-the-roof-likely-made-of-in-mark-24

humidity (water) reacts with the Earth mined salt. When Earth salt is carelessly stored it would lose its flavor. When this happened the Earth, salt was thrown on the roof tops of houses. Men and women working on the roof tops, and children playing on the roof tops would trample the salt under their feet.

The Hebrew Scriptures tell us that God called Israel to be a nation of spiritual leaders for all nations. The prophets that God sent to Israel tried to help the nation each time it lost its way and when that happened the Gentile nations of the earth would trample them (invade and exile the people). Like the prophets of the past Yeshua was warning the people not to allow themselves to stray from their spiritual mission from God. Israel was to be the living examples of the Kingdom of God no matter what the world's condition. Just because the people were being persecuted by the Romans, the people were to continue to be the spiritual leaders to the world.[13]

3. What is the symbolism of being the light of the world? (v. 14)

    The Aramaic word for light is *noohra*. This word metaphorically means "teaching, enlightenment, brilliance, intelligence." In the Middle East good and pious people were referred to as "light." The Torah and the teachings of the prophets were also considered to be as "light." In addition, the people referred to God's presence as "light."

    In Yeshua's day the light of Israel was buried under so many commentaries and man-made ordinances that it was impossible for people to see God's light in them. Many religious teachers of the day pretended to be concerned about minor laws so

---

[13] Errico, Rocco A., and George M. Lamsa. "Chapter 5." *Aramaic Light on the Gospel of Matthew: A Commentary on the Teachings of Jesus from the Aramaic and Unchanged Near Eastern Customs*. Santa Fe, NM: Noohra Foundation, 2000. N. pag. Print.

that they might break the more important ones. Thus, while they were condemning others, they were able to escape condemnation for their behavior.

"Faith, forgiveness, humility, meekness, peace, justice, love and purity of heart are the 'light' of the human soul and needs to shine in the world." [14] When these things do shine through us we will truly see the kingdom of God. Yeshua's disciples were to show these attributes can teach others how to do so. This would be obtained by following the teachings of Yeshua.

4. Why is it better to let light shine? (v. 14 & 15)

It is better to let light shine because then one is living by the attributes that are described in the previous question. If everyone allowed the light to shine through them the world would be a much better place and the kingdom of God will arrive.

Culture and Linguistics Section
  Discussion

This section of the sermon on the Mount tell us that Yeshua did not come to create a church but rather to communicate God's Torah to us, just as the prophets did, but the difference is He was also going to demonstrate what the Torah was all about. To have a civilized society we must have rules of order. God gave us those rules of order, how to behave with one another, when he gave us the Torah. Unfortunately, during Yeshua's time many of his contemporaries were able to convince the people that the Torah meant something different than what God intended it to mean. Therefore, Yeshua came to correct that problem. He let the religious leaders of the day know that they were teachings false doctrines. Naturally these religious leaders became quite

---

[14] IBID.

upset because they liked showing public piety but then in their homes they were not pious at all. Therefore, we learn some more characteristics of the kingdom of heaven and we also learn that if we do not practice the virtues that the Lord has told us to do that we cannot participate or enter the kingdom of heaven.

Thoughts

Yeshua continues to tell us about the kingdom of heaven. To be a participant in the kingdom of heaven one must be following the Torah. This means that one practices: Faith, forgiveness, humility, meekness, peace, justice, love and purity of heart. Yeshua also told us that he did not come to create a new religion. An interesting question for the church would be how to justify itself as a new religion when Yeshua was clear that he did not come to create a new religion. Looking at history it was Paul who went out to the Gentiles and created a church that became separate from the followers of Yeshua that remained in the Jerusalem area. So, is the church illegitimate? According to Yeshua, it maybe because Yeshua said he came to fulfill the Torah and the words of the prophets.

Reflections

Yeshua told his disciples and followers in his day that there were people that were corrupting the understanding of the Torah creating meanings for the passages that fit their desires. That still applies today. There are many TV evangelists who are distorting the word of God for their own profit. In many of our churches, there are pastors who are offering Sunday sermons not based on the actual word but are placing their trust in theologians and commentators who 1900 years ago decided that Judaism was not the basis of this new religion called Christianity. That would explain why Christianity looks so foreign to Judaism. Yeshua said that he came to fulfill the Torah and the prophets. Yeshua said that he did not come to create a new religion. Therefore, the question comes up as to whether the messianic Jewish movement is the movement that Yeshua truly wanted? If this is true, then how does the modern-day church react?

Matthew 5:21-26

Language

New American Standard 1995	Koine Greek
21 "You have heard that the ancients were told, 'YOU SHALL NOT COMMIT MURDER ' and 'Whoever commits murder shall be liable to the court.' 22 "But I say to you that everyone who is angry with his brother shall be guilty before the court; and whoever says to his brother, 'You good-for-nothing,' shall be guilty before the supreme court; and whoever says, 'You fool,' shall be guilty *enough to go* into the fiery hell. 23 "Therefore if you are presenting your offering at the altar, and there remember that your brother has something against you, 24 leave your offering there before the altar and go; first be reconciled to your brother, and then come and present your offering. 25 "Make friends quickly with your opponent at law while you are with him on the way, so that your opponent may not hand you over to the judge, and the judge to the officer, and you be thrown into prison. 26 "Truly I say to you, you will not come out of there until you have paid up the last cent.	21 Ἠκούσατε ὅτι ἐρρέθη τοῖς ἀρχαίοις, Οὐ φονεύσεις· ὃς δ' ἂν φονεύσῃ, ἔνοχος ἔσται τῇ κρίσει· 22 ἐγὼ δὲ λέγω ὑμῖν ὅτι πᾶς ὁ ὀργιζόμενος τῷ ἀδελφῷ αὐτοῦ εἰκῇ ἔνοχος ἔσται τῇ κρίσει· ὃς δ' ἂν εἴπῃ τῷ ἀδελφῷ αὐτοῦ, Ῥακά, ἔνοχος ἔσται τῷ συνεδρίῳ· ὃς δ' ἂν εἴπῃ, Μωρέ, ἔνοχος ἔσται εἰς τὴν γέενναν τοῦ πυρός. 23 Ἐὰν οὖν προσφέρῃς τὸ δῶρόν σου ἐπὶ τὸ θυσιαστήριον, καὶ ἐκεῖ μνησθῇς ὅτι ὁ ἀδελφός σου ἔχει τι κατὰ σοῦ, 24 ἄφες ἐκεῖ τὸ δῶρόν σου ἔμπροσθεν τοῦ θυσιαστηρίου, καὶ ὕπαγε, πρῶτον διαλλάγηθι τῷ ἀδελφῷ σου, καὶ τότε ἐλθὼν πρόσφερε τὸ δῶρόν σου. 25 Ἴσθι εὐνοῶν τῷ ἀντιδίκῳ σου ταχύ, ἕως ὅτου εἶ ἐν τῇ ὁδῷ μετ' αὐτοῦ, μήποτέ σε παραδῷ ὁ ἀντίδικος τῷ κριτῇ, καὶ ὁ κριτής σε παραδῷ τῷ ὑπηρέτῃ, καὶ εἰς φυλακὴν βληθήσῃ. 26 Ἀμὴν λέγω σοι, οὐ μὴ ἐξέλθῃς ἐκεῖθεν, ἕως ἂν ἀποδῷς τὸν ἔσχατον κοδράντην.

Process of Discovery

Linguistics Section

Linguistic Structure

A [21] "You have heard that the ancients were told, 'YOU SHALL NOT COMMIT MURDER ' and 'Whoever commits murder shall be liable to the court.' [22] "But I say to you that everyone who is angry with his brother shall be guilty before the court; and whoever says to his brother, 'You good-for-nothing,' shall be guilty before the supreme court; and whoever says, 'You fool,' shall be guilty *enough to go* into the fiery hell.

> **B** [23] "Therefore if you are presenting your offering at the altar, and there remember that your brother has something against you, [24] leave your offering there before the altar and go; first be reconciled to your brother, and then come and present your offering.

A' [25] "Make friends quickly with your opponent at law while you are with him on the way, so that your opponent may not hand you over to the judge, and the judge to the officer, and you be thrown into prison. [26] "Truly I say to you, you will not come out of there until you have paid up the last cent.

Discussion

A simple chiasm is presented in this passage. The passage is usually titled "Concerning Anger" or "Dealing with anger," which comes from verse twenty-two.

Questioning the Passage

1. Who were the ancients? (v. 21)

    The ancients are probably a reference to the Israelites who first received the Ten Commandments from God through Moses. It could be viewed as Yeshua saying that this commandment meant one thing to the people of Moses' time but means a lot more in His day and for us. This thought is because Yeshua expanded the commandment of murder to include anger between two or more members of the community.

2. What does the commandment about murder have to do with anger? (v. 21)

A community cannot survive if the people who are a part of it are quarrelling with each other. If a community cannot get along with itself, then it is destined to die. Thus, the anger and disputes that can evolve in the community will "murder" itself. Yeshua could have been trying to teach this fact to the people. The Jewish people needed to work together if they were going to survive as a nation. For the early church disputes inside of the house churches and small Christian communities could destroy the community. In the bigger sense of the general church, history has proven that the church divides whenever groups cannot resolve their anger toward one another. The modern topic that is splitting the church is the question of sexuality and the Bible. This situation is dividing church denominations currently and it appears not to have an end. The church cannot survive if it is fighting against itself.

3. What is the meaning of the escalation of anger shown in verse twenty-two?

- Angry with his brother shall be guilty before the court
- 'You good-for-nothing,' shall be guilty before the supreme court
- 'You fool,' shall be guilty *enough to go* into the fiery hell

Yeshua is expanding the meaning of the commandment about murder to include anger, which can be consider "murder in the heart."[15] This means that it is the anger that burns in the heart against another person that eventually leads to committing the act of murder. Therefore, Yeshua says that the anger must be squelched before it manifests. This verse is an allegory demonstrating how the building up of anger in one's heart can lead to murder. Murder is a one-way ticket to hell, according to Yeshua. Therefore, the warning is to stop the anger before it is too late.

---

[15] Hagner, Donald A. Matthew 14-28: The WORD Commentary, Volume 33b. Grand Rapids: Zondervan, 2015.

4. What does giving an offering to God have to do with having a negative situation with another person? (v. 23-24)

Removing anger from one's heart is so important that Yeshua says that we cannot come before God with an offering. The offering would not be accepted by God. The negative force of anger is that strong that it negates the positive force that can be created by making a physical offering to God.

Verse Comparison on citations or proof text

1. [21] "You have heard that the ancients were told, 'YOU SHALL NOT COMMIT MURDER ' and 'Whoever commits murder shall be liable to the court.' (Matt. 5:21 NAU)

The proof text for this verse is:

[13] "You shall not murder. (Exod. 20:13 NAU)

The verse directly quotes the murder commandment of the Ten Commandments.

Scripture cross references

Verse 21   Exo 20:13; Deu 5:17, Deu 16:18; 2Ch 19:5f

Verse 25   Pro 25:8f; Luk 12:58

Culture Section

Discussion

Settling disputes with adversaries was important. Semitic people preferred to settle their differences by arbitration or through peacemakers of the town. When that failed they would seek out government officials or judges. However, for most people they would have to travel to a judge. While on the way to the judge the difference was usually settled. Being away from friends and enemies allowed for an exchange of thoughts without any interference. If the dispute was not settled, they would come before a judge who could rule against both parties. Since judges were not paid and could be bribed, justice generally went to the wealthiest.

Thoughts

Yeshua knew that anger between people caused a division among them and it weakened the community of the people. In Yeshua's day there was a splintering of Judaism into several groups. Pharisees, Sadducees, Zealots and the Essence as the main groups of His day. These groups separated from each other because of arguments over the meaning of the Scripture and how to deal with the Roman occupation. The Jewish nation would have been stronger if it rid itself of its anger toward each other and remembered that they were the chosen people of the LORD. What were they showing the Romans when they could not get along with themselves.? Why is it that humans cannot coexist with each other even with differing views? Why do we let our differences become anger, which in most cases overtakes us and causes us to fight among ourselves? Perhaps the Jewish nation could have prevented the Roman occupation if they worked together as one nation by riding themselves of their anger toward each other.

Reflections

When will the church learn this lesson? Jesus was clear that anger separates us from each other and leads to murder. In Jesus' analysis of the commandment about murder, He included the nation of the people in the same category as murdering a person. The church has not been dealing with anger from the very beginning. Paul set out and decided to convert Mithras churches and established what he wanted to have happen. Today's church structure started with Paul saying that the house churches needed Bishops to oversee them. In 48 CE when the First Church Council came together the anger between Paul and Peter was apparent. They came to a consensus and all looked good for the church. However,

Paul left the council and decided not to abide by his agreement with Peter. If the theory that Paul converted Mithras churches is true, then what he agreed to at the church council could have destroyed the work that he had done. Therefore, Paul did what Paul wanted to do. Another view is that Paul was still angry with Peter who questioned him. From Paul's perspective he probably thought that since the Lord Jesus spoke to him on the Damascus road that what Paul was doing was what the Lord Jesus wanted. The bottom line is that the church divided in 48 CE and has been dividing ever since. The more the church divides the weaker it becomes. The anger between the Catholics and Protestants of today is proof of the anger that still boils from 500 years ago.

Look inside the church. The anger that exists on Sunday morning when the congregation comes together is clear. If you study the people and who they speak with, and how the speak, the anger between people in the church can be clearly mapped out.   The only way the church of Jesus Christ will survive into the 21st century and beyond is that the anger between Christians has to stop. Jesus commanded it and the disciples of today are not listening (just like our predecessors). Independent churches are growing because they were founded on the anger of a small group of people who left their mainline church. The new independent churches rid themselves of its anger by leaving the mainline church and become successful if they keep the anger out.

The mainline churches could learn from the breakaway independent churches by ridding its members of their internal anger toward one another. Our small dying churches eventually rid themselves of their anger by attrition. Eventually these small dying churches become anger free, but the membership is so small that any disturbance, like a roof replacement, which costs more than the church's resources, causes them to close. So, what is killing our churches? ANGER toward each other.

Anger is caused by disagreements over the way money is spent, the spiritual direction of the church, and the supported missions of the church. There are probably a lot more reasons that could be listed. The church resolution to anger and disputes is to push the problem under the rug and never to speak of it. Eventually the anger swells up and the splitting of the church begins. One side of the argument or the other leaves the church when it has determined that it cannot win. This is what Jesus is warning His church about.

Why does the church congregation not heed the words of Jesus? Many churches and followers of Jesus do not follow His words. In the case of anger, it is because they are egocentric people who must have their way all the times without compromise. It is because the church people who have been in the church forever like their traditional ways of doing things and the yearly cycle of events. They do not want to change or even have new ways added to "their" church. Note that they are not saying "Christ's church." They get angry at the younger generation who wants more and different things from the church. They demonstrate their anger toward the newer attendees until they drive them away. Then the angry church complains to the pastor that their church is shrinking. Many times, the angry church decides it is all the pastor's fault. Why? Because they certainly cannot blame themselves.

The solution is to rid the church of all its members' anger. This solution is something that a pastor cannot do by him/herself. It is up to the leadership of the church to determine what they will do about the angry individuals. For example, an independent church decided to expand itself by merging with another independent church. The people voted 90% in favor of the merge. The leadership decided to move forward on the merge. The Senior Pastor of this independent church, in a sermon, told the church that the merge was moving forward, and he politely told the people who were angry about the merge if they could not get on board with the church leadership that they needed to leave the church. Also, people who "bad mouthed" the decision or the new merged church were told to leave. Their solution removed the anger from the church.

For the church to survive its leadership must become bold about dealing with the anger in the church. Jesus says get rid of it.

Chapter 5:27-37

Language

New American Standard 1995	Koine Greek
21 "You have heard that the ancients were told, 'YOU SHALL NOT COMMIT MURDER ' and 'Whoever commits murder shall be liable to the court.' "But I say to you that everyone who is angry with his brother shall be guilty before the court; and whoever says to his brother, 'You good-for-nothing,' shall be guilty before the supreme court; and whoever says, 'You fool,' shall be guilty *enough to go* into the fiery hell. 23 "Therefore if you are presenting your offering at the altar, and there remember that your brother has something against you, 24 leave your offering there before the altar and go; first be reconciled to your brother, and then come and present your offering. 25 "Make friends quickly with your opponent at law while you are with him on the way, so that your opponent may not hand you over to the judge, and the judge to the officer, and you be thrown into prison. 26 "Truly I say to you, you will not come out of there until you have paid up the last cent.	21 Ἠκούσατε ὅτι ἐρρέθη τοῖς ἀρχαίοις, Οὐ φονεύσεις· ὃς δ' ἂν φονεύσῃ, ἔνοχος ἔσται τῇ κρίσει· 22 ἐγὼ δὲ λέγω ὑμῖν ὅτι πᾶς ὁ ὀργιζόμενος τῷ ἀδελφῷ αὐτοῦ εἰκῇ ἔνοχος ἔσται τῇ κρίσει· ὃς δ' ἂν εἴπῃ τῷ ἀδελφῷ αὐτοῦ, Ῥακά, ἔνοχος ἔσται τῷ συνεδρίῳ· ὃς δ' ἂν εἴπῃ, Μωρέ, ἔνοχος ἔσται εἰς τὴν γέενναν τοῦ πυρός. 23 Ἐὰν οὖν προσφέρῃς τὸ δῶρόν σου ἐπὶ τὸ θυσιαστήριον, καὶ ἐκεῖ μνησθῇς ὅτι ὁ ἀδελφός σου ἔχει τι κατὰ σοῦ, 24 ἄφες ἐκεῖ τὸ δῶρόν σου ἔμπροσθεν τοῦ θυσιαστηρίου, καὶ ὕπαγε, πρῶτον διαλλάγηθι τῷ ἀδελφῷ σου, καὶ τότε ἐλθὼν πρόσφερε τὸ δῶρόν σου. 25 Ἴσθι εὐνοῶν τῷ ἀντιδίκῳ σου ταχύ, ἕως ὅτου εἶ ἐν τῇ ὁδῷ μετ' αὐτοῦ, μήποτέ σε παραδῷ ὁ ἀντίδικος τῷ κριτῇ, καὶ ὁ κριτής σε παραδῷ τῷ ὑπηρέτῃ, καὶ εἰς φυλακὴν βληθήσῃ. 26 Ἀμὴν λέγω σοι, οὐ μὴ ἐξέλθῃς ἐκεῖθεν, ἕως ἂν ἀποδῷς τὸν ἔσχατον κοδράντην. 27 Ἠκούσατε ὅτι ἐρρέθη, Οὐ μοιχεύσεις· 28 ἐγὼ δὲ λέγω ὑμῖν, ὅτι πᾶς ὁ βλέπων γυναῖκα πρὸς τὸ ἐπιθυμῆσαι αὐτὴν ἤδη ἐμοίχευσεν αὐτὴν ἐν τῇ καρδίᾳ αὐτοῦ.

27 "You have heard that it was said, 'YOU SHALL NOT COMMIT ADULTERY';

28 but I say to you that everyone who looks at a woman with lust for her has already committed adultery with her in his heart.

29 "If your right eye makes you stumble, tear it out and throw it from you; for it is better for you to lose one of the parts of your body, than for your whole body to be thrown into hell.

30 "If your right hand makes you stumble, cut it off and throw it from you; for it is better for you to lose one of the parts of your body, than for your whole body to go into hell.

31 "It was said, 'WHOEVER SENDS HIS WIFE AWAY, LET HIM GIVE HER A CERTIFICATE OF DIVORCE';

32 but I say to you that everyone who divorces his wife, except for *the* reason of unchastity, makes her commit adultery; and whoever marries a divorced woman commits adultery.

33 "Again, you have heard that the ancients were told, 'YOU SHALL NOT MAKE FALSE VOWS, BUT SHALL FULFILL YOUR VOWS TO THE LORD.'

34 "But I say to you, make no oath at all, either by heaven, for it is the throne of God,

35 or by the earth, for it is the footstool of His feet, or by Jerusalem, for it is THE CITY OF THE GREAT KING.

36 "Nor shall you make an oath by your head, for you cannot make one hair white or black.

29 Εἰ δὲ ὁ ὀφθαλμός σου ὁ δεξιὸς σκανδαλίζει σε, ἔξελε αὐτὸν καὶ βάλε ἀπὸ σοῦ· συμφέρει γάρ σοι ἵνα ἀπόληται ἓν τῶν μελῶν σου, καὶ μὴ ὅλον τὸ σῶμά σου βληθῇ εἰς γέενναν.

30 Καὶ εἰ ἡ δεξιά σου χείρ σκανδαλίζει σε, ἔκκοψον αὐτὴν καὶ βάλε ἀπὸ σοῦ· συμφέρει γάρ σοι ἵνα ἀπόληται ἓν τῶν μελῶν σου, καὶ μὴ ὅλον τὸ σῶμά σου βληθῇ εἰς γέενναν.

31 Ἐρρέθη δὲ ὅτι Ὃς ἂν ἀπολύσῃ τὴν γυναῖκα αὐτοῦ, δότω αὐτῇ ἀποστάσιον·

32 ἐγὼ δὲ λέγω ὑμῖν, ὅτι ὃς ἂν ἀπολύσῃ τὴν γυναῖκα αὐτοῦ, παρεκτὸς λόγου πορνείας, ποιεῖ αὐτὴν μοιχᾶσθαι· καὶ ὃς ἐὰν ἀπολελυμένην γαμήσῃ μοιχᾶται.

33 Πάλιν ἠκούσατε ὅτι ἐρρέθη τοῖς ἀρχαίοις, Οὐκ ἐπιορκήσεις, ἀποδώσεις δὲ τῷ κυρίῳ τοὺς ὅρκους σου·

34 ἐγὼ δὲ λέγω ὑμῖν μὴ ὀμόσαι ὅλως· μήτε ἐν τῷ οὐρανῷ, ὅτι θρόνος ἐστὶν τοῦ θεοῦ·

35 μήτε ἐν τῇ γῇ, ὅτι ὑποπόδιόν ἐστιν τῶν ποδῶν αὐτοῦ· μήτε εἰς Ἱεροσόλυμα, ὅτι πόλις ἐστὶν τοῦ μεγάλου βασιλέως·

36 μήτε ἐν τῇ κεφαλῇ σου ὀμόσῃς, ὅτι οὐ δύνασαι μίαν τρίχα λευκὴν ἢ μέλαιναν ποιῆσαι.

37 Ἔστω δὲ ὁ λόγος ὑμῶν, ναὶ ναί, οὒ οὔ· τὸ δὲ περισσὸν τούτων ἐκ τοῦ πονηροῦ ἐστιν.

<table>
<tr><td>

[37] "But let your statement be, 'Yes, yes ' *or* 'No, no'; anything beyond these is of evil.

</td><td></td></tr>
</table>

Process of Discovery

Linguistics Section

Linguistic Structure

A [27] "You have heard that it was said, 'YOU SHALL NOT COMMIT ADULTERY'; [28] but I say to you that everyone who looks at a woman with lust for her has already committed adultery with her in his heart.

    B [29] "If your right eye makes you stumble, tear it out and throw it from you; for it is better for you to lose one of the parts of your body, than for your whole body to be thrown into hell.

    B1 [30] "If your right hand makes you stumble, cut it off and throw it from you; for it is better for you to lose one of the parts of your body, than for your whole body to go into hell.

A' [31] "It was said, 'WHOEVER SENDS HIS WIFE AWAY, LET HIM GIVE HER A CERTIFICATE OF DIVORCE'; [32] but I say to you that everyone who divorces his wife, except for *the* reason of unchastity, makes her commit adultery; and whoever marries a divorced woman commits adultery.

    A: The teaching about the sin of adultery. B: Parables about parts of one's body[16]

A [33] "Again, you have heard that the ancients were told, 'YOU SHALL NOT MAKE FALSE VOWS, BUT SHALL FULFILL YOUR VOWS TO THE LORD.' [34] "But I say to you, make no oath at all,

    B either by heaven, for it is the throne of God,

    B1 [35] or by the earth, for it is the footstool of His feet, or by Jerusalem, for it is THE CITY OF THE GREAT KING.

---

[16] IBID.

B2 [36] "Nor shall you make an oath by your head, for you cannot make one hair white or black.

A' [37] "But let your statement be, 'Yes, yes ' *or* 'No, no'; anything beyond these is of evil.[17]

Questioning the Passage

This section of the Sermon on the Mount needs to be examined with respect to the culture. Therefore, the culture and language of this passage is examined block by block in the cultural section.

Translation Inconsistencies

[22] "But I say to you that everyone who is angry with his brother (Matt. 5:22 NAU)

According to Rocco Errico, the Aramaic word *raca* was not translated into Greek. Therefore, the English version does not contain this word.

"and whosoever shall say to his brother Raca, shall be in danger of the council" (Peshitta)

Raqa means "to spit." Some men in Yeshua's day would kill someone who spoke such a word or who would spit in another's face.[18]

---

[17] IBID.

[18] Errico, Rocco A., and George M. Lamsa. "Chapter 5." *Aramaic Light on the Gospel of Matthew: A Commentary on the Teachings of Jesus from the Aramaic and Unchanged Near Eastern Customs*. Santa Fe, NM: Noohra Foundation, 2000. N. pag. Print.

Culture Section

[Matthew 5:27-28] Voyeurism

Lust had a different meaning in Yeshua's day. Near Eastern woman always covered their faces with a veil. They did not appreciate non-family men looking at them. Some women were so shy they would wear their veil in the presence of their husbands. Men and women seldom meet socially. Therefore, a woman's body was a mystery to men. This caused men would secretly desire to look at a women. "Looking at a woman" did not mean to look at her face but rather to try to see her body. When women bathed the men would hide themselves on the rooftops to get a glance of a naked woman. That is what King David was doing with Bathsheba. Doing so could illicit an adulterous affair (like David). It is this kind of "looking at a woman" that Yeshua was referring to. In western culture we would say "don't be a peeping Tom."

[Matthew 5:29-30] The Eye and the Hand

In Yeshua's day the eye was a symbol of desire and envy. There are many superstitions in the Semitic world about the eye. The idea of the "evil eye" comes from the Middle East. The expression "cut your eye from my boy," means, "don't envy my boy." The expression "do not cut your eye from my family while I am away," means "look after my family while I am absent from them." If a woman has a reputation of having the "evil eye" enters a home where there is a handsome lad, the lad's mother would smear his face with charcoal to avoid the spell of the evil eye. To look at a baby or child and say "what a beautiful child" is thought to bring the evil eye (of envy) upon the child. Instead the person would say "what an ugly child." The faces of children were kept dirty to ward off the evil eye.

"Pluck out the envying and coveting eye" is an Aramaic idiom. This means if you are envious of another persons' property it is imperative to stop the habit before the envy brings you to steal the property. It is better to lose an eye than to become a slave to envy.

Semitic people deemed the right side of the body, eye, hand, foot, as more important than the left side. "Cutting off your hand" is an Aramaic saying. It is not referring to the actual cutting off of the hand. Rather it means that a person must prevent themselves from doing any kind of evil. "Cut off your hand from my vineyard" means "don't gather grapes from my vineyard. "His hand is too long" refers to a thief. "Shorten your hand: means "do not steal." The meaning of plucking and cutting off is to stop a bad habit.

Falling into hell means that performing an evil act of which involves the hand or eye is greater than the loss of the hand or eye. "Hell," metaphorically means "mental suffering, anguish, and regret." The term Hell is not understood literally in the Near East. Western Christianity came to understand Hell as a place of bodily torment by fire. For the Near Easterner Hell is a place of mental agony and mental suffering. It was believed that mental anguish continues forever while being burned is a short-term punishment.

[Mathew 5:31-32] Divorce

Near Eastern people do not recognize nor practice civil marriages. The bond between a man and woman in marriage comes from the priest and the payment of a dowry. Marriage is considered a sacred institution and is never mixed with politics or courts. Women view marriage as a lottery because the marriages are prearranged, and they have no say in whom they will marry. The sole authority in a marriage is with the husband, who can exercise unlimited power over his wife or wives.

Men can divorce their wife for not bearing children, for not working hard enough (according to his standard) and were considered and treated as property. Divorce became so easy in Yeshua's day that religious laws had to be instituted.

Yeshua condemned the laxity of the divorce laws of His day and wanted to strengthen them. Yeshua was against the practice of men divorcing their wives for arbitrary reasons. He also saw how husbands would mistreat their wives. Yeshua believed in the equality of men and women. Therefore, He believed that a woman was not be divorced except for the grounds of adultery.

[Matthew 5:33-37] Swearing

Swearing an oath to God, holy men, and sacred places was an integral element in Semitic speech. The Scripture is filled with such oaths. It was very natural for a speaker to turn his eyes and lift his hand toward Heaven and say, "By God, what I said is right and true!" By the time of Yeshua this swearing of oaths had lost its original sacredness and became meaningless. Yeshua encouraged truthful and straightforward conversation instead of offering oaths that had no value.

People took oaths in the name of God and the Temple because they believed in sacred oaths and in a Higher Power, but they swore falsely. They were using the name of the LORD to cover their dishonest actions. This caused the culture of swearing to become a useless practice. What value is there to an oath of a liar? Yeshua tells us to talk with directness and frankness when dealing with one another. He also knew that if a man is cheated he will be encouraged to cheat someone else.

"Yes, yes and no, no" is the only successful and straightforward method in doing business. It means no swearing, no oaths, no promises.

Thoughts

A practical way to express this view is by summarizing each section.

[Matthew 5:27-28] Voyeurism

Lust   Lust had a different meaning in Yeshua's day

Near Eastern women always covered their body and faces

The women did not appreciate non-family men looking at them

Therefore, a woman's body was a mystery to men

Of course, men secretly wanted to take a look

When women bathed in the center courtyard, men would hide themselves on the rooftops, in an attempt to, see the naked women (King David is a good example)

This practice could (and did) lead to adultery

"Peeping Tom"

[Matthew 5:29-30] The Eye and the Hand

Eye   Was a symbol of desire and envy

Many superstitions about the eye

"Evil eye"

"Cut your eye from my boy" means "don't envy my boy"

If a woman with the evil eye entered a home the mother of a handsome lad would smear his face with charcoal to avoid the evil eye

To say "what a beautiful child" was thought to bring the evil eye

Instead one would say "what an ugly child"

Pluck out   If you are envious of another you must stop it before you are inclined

                  to steal property

              Between to lose an eye than to become a slave to envy

Right side   The right side of the body, hand, eye, foot, etc., was considered more

                  important than the left side

              "Cutting off your hand" means a person must prevent themselves

                  from doing any evil

              "His hand is too long" refers to a thief

              "Shorten your hand" means do not steal

              Cutting or plucking off a body part means to stop a bad habit

Falling into hellMeans that performing an evil act which involved the hand or eye is

                  greater than the loss of the hand or eye

              Hell metaphorically means "mental suffering, anguish and regret

              Hell for Near Easterner is a place of continual mental suffering and

                  anguish which continues forever (not a place of fire and torture

                  as Western Christianity has made it

[Matthew 5:31-32] Divorce

Marriage   Religious only marriage

              Priest, vows and dowry

              Sacred Institution

              Women saw it as a lottery

              Prearranged marriages

              Husband was sole authority

              Men could divorce because: no children, not working hard enough

> Divorce was easy for a man
>
> Strengthening the divorce laws
>
> Women equal to men

[Matthew 5:33-37] Swearing

Oath   Swearing oaths was common

       Oaths sworn in the name of God

       Many oaths created to cover up other evils

       Straight forward talk is better than oaths

       An oath of a liar is worthless

Reflections

With respect to Hell, most people find this idea a difficult concept because they do not believe in an eternal punishment. However, the Scripture do teach about this place. In the Zohar two areas of Hell are described. Sheol is the place where eternal punishment occurs. Avadon is where one can repent for one's sins and eventually reach Heaven. Yom Kippur is the day of each year when a person can repent to the LORD for all sins committed during the previous year. With respect to lust the view is that anything that can give rise to adultery is considered sinful. Divorce is treated as a sin but is forgivable as all other sins are. Of course, any discourse between people should be attended to as soon as possible and cleared up. As Yeshua said one should forgive those who sin against another.

Matthew 5:38-42

Language

New American Standard 1995	Koine Greek
[38] "You have heard that it was said, 'AN EYE FOR AN EYE, AND A TOOTH FOR A TOOTH.' [39] "But I say to you, do not resist an evil person; but whoever slaps you on your right cheek, turn the other to him also. [40] "If anyone wants to sue you and take your shirt, let him have your coat also. [41] "Whoever forces you to go one mile, go with him two. [42] "Give to him who asks of you, and do not turn away from him who wants to borrow from you.	[8] Ἠκούσατε ὅτι ἐρρέθη, Ὀφθαλμὸν ἀντὶ ὀφθαλμοῦ, καὶ ὀδόντα ἀντὶ ὀδόντος· [39] ἐγὼ δὲ λέγω ὑμῖν μὴ ἀντιστῆναι τῷ πονηρῷ· ἀλλ' ὅστις σε ῥαπίσει ἐπὶ τὴν δεξιὰν σιαγόνα, στρέψον αὐτῷ καὶ τὴν ἄλλην· [40] καὶ τῷ θέλοντί σοι κριθῆναι καὶ τὸν χιτῶνά σου λαβεῖν, ἄφες αὐτῷ καὶ τὸ ἱμάτιον· [41] καὶ ὅστις σε ἀγγαρεύσει μίλιον ἕν, ὕπαγε μετ' αὐτοῦ δύο. [42] Τῷ αἰτοῦντί σε δίδου· καὶ τὸν θέλοντα ἀπὸ σοῦ δανείσασθαι μὴ ἀποστραφῇς.

Process of Discovery

Linguistics Section

Linguistic Structure

A [38] "You have heard that it was said, 'AN EYE FOR AN EYE, AND A TOOTH FOR A TOOTH.' [39] "But I say to you, do not resist an evil person;

B1 but whoever slaps you on your right cheek, turn the other to him also.
B2 [40] "If anyone wants to sue you and take your shirt, let him have your coat also.
B3 [41] "Whoever forces you to go one mile, go with him two.

A' [42] "Give to him who asks of you, and do not turn away from him who wants to borrow from you.

Discussion

This passage forms a simple chiasm A-B-A' with several focal points. The three "B" blocks deal with retaliation against someone who has done a person wrong. This be a corollary to the commandment to "love your neighbor."

Questioning the Passage

1. What is the purpose of this passage?

   Yeshua gave us the commandment to love each other. He is expanding this definition in chapter five. If you love your neighbor and are wronged by him, then justice should prevail. The punishment should equal the crime and not more.

2. How does Yeshua classify retaliation?

   A purpose of Yeshua's mission was to bring back the kingdom of Heaven to Earth. Having unlimited revenge is not a way of the Kingdom of God but rather it is a main part of the Kingdom of Satan. Violence in any form can be considered satanic. Thus, as followers of Yeshua we must be on our guard not to extract revenge. Justice for a crime is one thing. This is within the Kingdom of Heaven. Revenge is a part of the Kingdom of Satan. Many Christian theologians over the centuries interpreted this passage as Yeshua saying that when one is wronged that forgiveness should occur, which is correct, but that justice for the crime does not have to occur.

3. What does it mean "to turn the other cheek" in verse 39?

   Yeshua tells us that when wronged that revenge is not to be taken. Turning the other cheek is saying that justice can be done for the crime but nothing more. Yeshua is not saying that one must become a "door mat." Rather, He is saying that revenge is wrong.

Obtain justice but not retaliation. To seek revenge is a selfish pursuit and will cause a person to do more than seek retribution.[19]

Another view of this verse is that in ancient times a backhanded blow to the face was to insult the person. From this point of view Yeshua is saying that it is better to accept the insult and not give an insult back. If one responds to an insult with an insult it could escalate into something worse. Followers of Yeshua know that insults are just words.

4. Why would you give your coat away if someone is suing you? (v. 40)

Yeshua does not want us to take this verse literally. Why? Because if you were standing in a courtroom and gave away your shirt and coat you would be standing naked. The allegorical meaning is that we need to trust in the LORD to ensure that our rights under the Torah will be administrated.

Verse Comparison on citations or proof text

1. [38] "You have heard that it was said, 'AN EYE FOR AN EYE, AND A TOOTH FOR A TOOTH.'

   [23] "But if there is *any further* injury, then you shall appoint *as a penalty* life for life, [24] eye for eye, tooth for tooth, hand for hand, foot for foot, [25] burn for burn, wound for wound, bruise for bruise. (Exod. 21:23-25 NAU)

Scripture cross references

Verse 38   Exo 21:24; Lev 24:20; Deu 19:21

Verse 39   Exo 21:24; Lev 24:20; Deu 19:21

---

[19] The New Interpreter's Bible Commentary. Nashville: Abingdon Press, 1995.

Linguistic Echoes

A linguistic echo is found for verse 38 from Genesis 4:23-24 which can be viewed as the LORD telling us that unlimited private revenge is not acceptable. A person who is wronged must not take revenge against the person who wronged him. Rather he must seek the LORD's justice.

> [23] Lamech said to his wives, "Adah and Zillah, Listen to my voice, You wives of Lamech, Give heed to my speech, For I have killed a man for wounding me; And a boy for striking me; [24] If Cain is avenged sevenfold, Then Lamech seventy-sevenfold." (Gen. 4:23-24 NAU)

A second linguistic echo is found for verse 40 from Exodus 22:25-26. It is not legal to take a person's clock and keep up beyond sunset. However, if the cloak is given away then it is legal.

> [26] "If you ever take your neighbor's cloak as a pledge, you are to return it to him before the sun sets, [27] for that is his only covering; it is his cloak for his body. (Exod. 22:26-27 NAU)

Rules of Hillel

This passage is an expansion of the commandment to "love your neighbor." It gives more definition to this commandment.

Mishnah

In this passage Yeshua is saying that the LORD commands us not to take revenge because of a wrong doing. "Retribution and punishment must be commensurate with the crime; contrast Cain and Lamech's extraction of multiplied vengeance at Genesis 4:24"[20] The following citation is Bava Kama 8:1 from the Mishnah, which shows the rabbinic thinking about retaliation in Yeshua's time.

---

[20] Stern, David H. Jewish New Testament Commentary: A Companion Volume to the Jewish New Testament. Clarksville, MD: Jewish New Testament Publications, 1999. (Stern 1999)

One who injures his fellow is liable concerning him for five categories [of payment]: damages, pain, healthcare, unemployment, and shame. For damages, how [is this calculated?] One who puts out his eye, cuts off his hand, breaks his leg—we see him as if he were a slave sold in the marketplace, and we evaluate how much he was worth [the injury] and how much he is worth now. Pain? When he burned him with a spit or a nail—even on his fingernail—anything where there is no [permanent] wound, we evaluate how much a similar person would want to pay to be spared this [pain]. Healthcare? When he strikes him, he is liable for his healthcare costs. If swellings arose on him, if they were because of the strike, then he is liable; but if it was not because of the strike, he is exempt. If the swelling healed and then reopened and then healed and reopened, he is liable for his healthcare. If it healed entirely, he is exempt from his healing. Unemployment? We see him as if he were a guard of gourds, since he already gave him the value [for the loss] of his hand or his leg. Shame? All depends on the one who shames and the one who is shamed. One who shames a naked person, a blind person or a sleeping person is liable. If a sleeping person embarrasses, he is exempt. One who falls from the roof and caused damage and shamed, he is liable for damages and exempt for shame, as it is written, "[when two men fight and the wife of one comes out to save her husband,] and she puts out her hand and seizes his genitals (lit. damages his shame) [you shall cut off her hand]" (Deuteronomy 25:11-12). No one is liable for shame unless one intended to cause it.[21]

---

[21] "A Living Library of Jewish Texts ספריה חיה של טקסטים יהודיים." Kol Isha: Source Sheet Based on Rav Mosheh Lichtenstein's Article in Tradition | Sefaria Source Sheet Builder. Accessed July 11, 2018. https://www.sefaria.org/. (A Living Library of Jewish Texts n.d.)

Culture Section

Discussion

[Matthew 5:38-39]

The interpretation of the Mosaic Law was done when Israel was wandering through the wilderness for 40 years and had established itself as a semi-nomadic group of people even when they reach the Promised Land. They were illiterate people and uncultured therefore, they created harsh penalties for breaking the law. It was the unruly behavior of people lying, quarreling, and stealing from one another that caused Moses to implement such harsh penalties.

First century living in the days of Yeshua was quite different. The people in Judea were educated and aware of God's word. In most towns they were synagogues and rabbis to teach the word of God to the people and they constantly were reading the Torah and the words of the prophets. They also understood recompensing evil for evil only caused evil to multiply and increase. When evil increased hatred and vengeance would result, and murder and injuries would occur. Therefore, offering an eye for an eye was no longer a good solution. Yeshua understood that if one does not resist evil or react to evil that it diminishes the power of evil.

In verse 39 the word evil refers to an injustice. Middle Eastern people were forced into hard labor. We can see this in the Hebrew Scriptures when after Solomon died the people revolted against Solomon's forced harsh labor and the kingdom divided. Those who are in power generally oppressed the poor because the poor could not fight back. Nonresistance is a weapon that the poor can use to defend themselves. Politicians, government officials and the rich were always friendly and kind to those who would do the hard labor for them. The people who resisted were treated as rebels and traitors and were made to pay a heavy penalties. Therefore, resistance to Roman officials and soldiers who were misusing their authority was futile.

The phrase "turning the other cheek" is an Aramaic idiom which means "learn to take the wind out of the other person's sails," or "settle a problem while it is small." This verse has been used through the church to mean that we should be passive, rather Yeshua meant it to be a remedy against strife and vengeance. Yeshua did not restrict our need for self-defense.[22]

[Matthew 5:40]

During Yeshua's day they were petty bandits and robbers who would take a victim's garments and even their shoes by force. Clothing was frequently stolen from homes because they were considered of high value. When a person was suspected of a crime their good upper garments were used as a bail bond. If a person was found guilty of a crime or owing money to another person and they had no money, they were stripped of their clothes and their clothes were given to the person they owed the money.

Creditors also accept clothing as collateral for loans. If a person failed to pay back their loan the creditor was always willing to accept garments in lieu of payment. In Yeshua's day Near Easterners wore many undergarments and robes, one over the other in summer and winter alike. The more clothing a man wore the higher his social status. Therefore, if he had to relinquish his outer garment he would not go naked because of the layers of clothing he wore underneath.

---

[22] Errico, Rocco A., and George M. Lamsa. "Chapter 5." *Aramaic Light on the Gospel of Matthew: A Commentary on the Teachings of Jesus from the Aramaic and Unchanged Near Eastern Customs*. Santa Fe, NM: Noohra Foundation, 2000. N. pag. Print.

What Yeshua was saying here is that we need to be willing to work out our differences. In his day one would do this by saying "you may have my undergarment also."[23]

[Matthew 5:41]

In Yeshua's day merchandise, food supplies, and building materials were carried on the backs of animals and men. In some of the isolated regions of the country where animals were scarce, men and women would carry supplies on their backs 20 or more miles. When army regiments moved from place to place, they would draft men and animals to carry their supplies. The Army officers would divide the work among the people who they recruited from the towns that were on route to their destination. People would carry supplies from one town to the next. In the Galilee and Judea many of the towns were less than 1 mile to 2 miles apart.

When the Army officers went into a town and asked for volunteers those who gladly responded to the summons and willing to carry supplies were released as soon as they arrived in the next town. But if not, enough volunteers came forward the Army officers would forcibly recruit men to carry their supplies. Those who resisted or failed to show up at the proper time to carry the supplies would be forced to carry supplies for two to three days instead of just going one or two miles. The general reply to an Army officer was "I will be glad to go to miles, my Lord." To these people the officers would give them a lighter burden and release them sooner.

Yeshua knew that nonresistance was the only way to combat mistreatment from others. Being meek and gentle brought less mistreatment than resistance did.[24]

---

[23] IBID.
[24] IBID.

[Matthew 5:42]

We can show care and compassion to our neighbors by sharing what we have with them especially when they are in a time of need. Yeshua was simply saying that we need to learn to share what we have with others. There is a near Eastern saying, "do not refuse your neighbor's request, for tomorrow you may be in want."[25]

Thoughts

This section of the Sermon on the Mount is Yeshua expanding the definition of what loving your neighbor means. Three examples are given about not taking retaliation against someone who has hurt you. Justice will be performed. If justice cannot be performed in the society then it will be done by the LORD.

Why is it that Yeshua must deeply explain what it means to "love your neighbor?" It seems so straight forward. Perhaps it is because people do not want to follow the ways of the LORD. Several years ago, I received an email from a parishioner in the church I was serving asking me to tell him where in the Bible it says that one is not allowed to hate. My first thought was "are you kidding?" The question was from a long time Christian who regularly attended church. The emotion of hatred is completely opposite the emotion to love. To hate someone means that you cannot love them. Yeshua does not say "do not hate" but rather He says, "love everyone." I did find the command not to hate people in 1 John. The question was incredible. Therefore, I can see why Yeshua had spell out what love your neighbor means. Perhaps He should have also said "do not hate any person."

---

[25] IBID.

Justice is something that our society is permitted to do. Evil inclination infects people all the time and is supported by Satan. Since evil exists society must have rules and regulations regarding injustices. Yeshua is not saying that justice should not be served, rather He is saying that more than an appropriate about of justice should not prevail. Also, we need to remember that if society does not offer the proper level of justice then the LORD will. At times that does not give a satisfactory feeling to the person who was wronged. Yeshua knew that it would be difficult to accept this condition. However, Yeshua has faith in His disciples to obey His words.

Reflections

If a bully is picking on me does this passage say that I am supposed to take it? The way Christian theologians have presented this passage through the years, the answer is yes. But that is not how our society works. If one is wronged the normal response is to want justice and at times revenge. Someone hurts you and you want to hurt them back. The law of "an eye for an eye, and a tooth for a tooth" says that the punishment must fit the crime. To resist evil means to not seek revenge, but rather to seek justice. Throughout the centuries Yeshua has become portrayed as a man of peace who accepts whatever is thrown at Him. But that is not what He was saying. Western/Greek thinking has determined that this passage tells us to be passive. If one is always passive then one will be used, abused and taken advantage of. The Semitic view is that justice should be done inside the community. The punishment must fit the crime. Taking revenge means that one will inflict more than just the punishment upon the offender. According to Yeshua that is wrong.

There are also times when it is better to just let a wrong go rather than to pursue justice. For example, a verbal insult is merely words and can be ignored. The old saying is "sticks and stones will break my bones, but names never hurt me." Evil people can use insults to provoke a person to anger and that can lead to violence.

The reference to "go with him two" in verse forty-one implies that life is not fair. In Yeshua's day it was referring to a command by the conquering army of Israel. Today it could be referring to the unfairness of society. For example: a seminary student was once told that he could not go on a cross cultural trip to Arizona and Mexico because part of the stay was inside a 1st world country. That same year the seminary cross cultural trip was to South Africa. South Africa is a 1st world country. The hypocrisy is glaring. The student had no choice but to turn to a different cross-cultural trip in a 3rd world country because he could not afford the trip to South Africa. He walked not one mile but two miles. The conditions were not fair. Yeshua tells us in several places in the Gospels that life is not fair. But since the student wanted to graduate and the cross-cultural trip was a requirement, he decided to walk the extra mile.

Life's not always fair and many times you have to accept it.

Matthew 5:43-48

Language

New American Standard 1995	Koine Greek
[43] "You have heard that it was said, 'YOU SHALL LOVE YOUR NEIGHBOR and hate your enemy.' [44] "But I say to you, love your enemies and pray for those who persecute you, [45] so that you may be sons of your Father who is in heaven; for He causes His sun to rise on *the* evil and *the* good, and sends rain on *the* righteous and *the* unrighteous. [46] "For if you love those who love you, what reward do you have? Do not even the tax collectors do the same? [47] "If you greet only your brothers, what more are you doing *than others*? Do not even the Gentiles do the same? [48] "Therefore you are to be perfect, as your heavenly Father is perfect.	[43] Ἠκούσατε ὅτι ἐρρέθη, Ἀγαπήσεις τὸν πλησίον σου, καὶ μισήσεις τὸν ἐχθρόν σου· [44] ἐγὼ δὲ λέγω ὑμῖν, Ἀγαπᾶτε τοὺς ἐχθροὺς ὑμῶν, εὐλογεῖτε τοὺς καταρωμένους ὑμᾶς, καλῶς ποιεῖτε τοῖς μισοῦσιν ὑμᾶς, καὶ προσεύχεσθε ὑπὲρ τῶν ἐπηρεαζόντων ὑμᾶς, καὶ διωκόντων ὑμᾶς· [45] ὅπως γένησθε υἱοὶ τοῦ πατρὸς ὑμῶν τοῦ ἐν τοῖς οὐρανοῖς, ὅτι τὸν ἥλιον αὐτοῦ ἀνατέλλει ἐπὶ πονηροὺς καὶ ἀγαθούς, καὶ βρέχει ἐπὶ δικαίους καὶ ἀδίκους. [46] Ἐὰν γὰρ ἀγαπήσητε τοὺς ἀγαπῶντας ὑμᾶς, τίνα μισθὸν ἔχετε; Οὐχὶ καὶ οἱ τελῶναι τὸ αὐτὸ ποιοῦσιν; [47] Καὶ ἐὰν ἀσπάσησθε τοὺς φίλους ὑμῶν μόνον, τί περισσὸν ποιεῖτε; Οὐχὶ καὶ οἱ τελῶναι οὕτως ποιοῦσιν; [48] Ἔσεσθε οὖν ὑμεῖς τέλειοι, ὥσπερ ὁ πατὴρ ὑμῶν ὁ ἐν τοῖς οὐρανοῖς τέλειός ἐστιν.

Process of Discovery

Linguistics Section

Linguistic Structure

A [43] "You have heard that it was said, 'YOU SHALL LOVE YOUR NEIGHBOR and hate your enemy.' [44] "But I say to you, love your enemies and pray for those who persecute you,

> **B** [45] so that you may be sons of your Father who is in heaven; for He causes His sun to rise on *the* evil and *the* good, and sends rain on *the* righteous and *the* unrighteous.

A' [46] "For if you love those who love you, what reward do you have? Do not even the tax collectors do the same? [47] "If you greet only your brothers, what more are you doing *than others*? Do not even the Gentiles do the same?

> **B'** [48] "Therefore you are to be perfect, as your heavenly Father is perfect.

A: About love. B: About the heavenly father.[26]

Discussion

This passage is a simple A-B-A'-B' chiasm. It is the conclusion of this section of the sermon on the Mount in which Yeshua speaks about what loving your neighbor is all about.

Questioning the Passage

1. Where in the Hebrew Scriptures does it say to hate your enemy? (v. 43)

   Nowhere in the Hebrew Scripture does it say to hate our enemy. This idea comes from a misinterpretation of the Scripture and is a man-made.

   > [2] "I have loved you," says the LORD. But you say, "How have You loved us?"

   > "*Was* not Esau Jacob's brother?" declares the LORD. "Yet I have loved Jacob;

---

[26] Murai, Hajime. "Literary Structure (chiasm, Chiasmus) of Gospel of Matthew." Literary Structure (chiasm, Chiasmus) of Each Pericopes of Gospel of John. Accessed July 24, 2018.
http://www.bible.literarystructure.info/bible/40_Matthew_pericope_e.html.

[3] but I have hated Esau, and I have made his mountains a desolation and *appointed* his inheritance for the jackals of the wilderness." (Mal. 1:2-3 NAU)

In the context of this verse the Hebrew word

שָׂנֵא

which can be translated as "hate" and is used to express God's displeasure with the descendants of Esau who turned away from the Lord and the covenant of Abraham. This occurred when Esau decided to marry a Canaanite women and his descendants decided not to serve the Lord. Therefore, a context translation of this word would be "displeased." The Hebrew Scripture never tells us that it is allowable to hate anyone.[27]

Therefore, the passage Matthew 5:43-47 is Yeshua correcting the believe that one can "hate your enemy."

2. What does it mean to be sons of your Father in heaven? (v. 45)
Yeshua is using this phrase to tell His disciples that if they want to be a part of the Kingdom of Heaven then they need to follow His commandments. When a person is a part of the Kingdom of Heaven then that person is a son or daughter of God the Father.

3. What are the allegories of verse 45 (the sun and rain) mean?
"One important foundation for the unheard-of command to love one's enemies is the very fact that God gives his good gifts of sunshine and rain both to good and too bad."[28] Yeshua reminds us that the rain and sunshine fall upon the righteous and the

---

[27] Stern, David H. Jewish New Testament Commentary: A Companion Volume to the Jewish New Testament. Clarksville, MD: Jewish New Testament Publications, 1999.
[28] Hagner, D. A. (1998). Matthew 1–13 (Vol. 33A, p. 134). Dallas: Word, Incorporated.

unrighteous. Yeshua wants the unrighteous to give up their evil ways and become members of the Kingdom of Heaven. As members of the Kingdom of Heaven Yeshua expects us to demonstrate the love of God to all people.

4. What does the reference to the tax collectors tell us? (v. 46)

    Tax collectors were Jewish collaborators in Yeshua's day. They were considered the most despised people in Judea. Yeshua is telling the people that they should pray for the collaborators that they will see the error of their ways and return to the Kingdom of Heaven.

5. Why should one greet strangers? (v. 47)

    A greeting in Yeshua's day was considered an expression of recognition but also a recognition that God was with that person. Hebrews did not, in general, greet Gentiles in a manner which shined God's love upon them. Yeshua is saying that the Gentiles should be blessed and are a part of the Kingdom of Heaven if they so wish to be. It is not any person's place to determine who is and who is not allowed in the Kingdom of Heaven. From our point of view, it is God who makes that determination.[29]

Verse Comparison on citations or proof text

1. [43] "You have heard that it was said, 'YOU SHALL LOVE YOUR NEIGHBOR and hate your enemy.' (Matt. 5:43 NAU)

    The commandment to love your neighbors comes from Leviticus 19:18.

---

[29] Hagner, D. A. (1998). Matthew 1–13 (Vol. 33A, p. 134). Dallas: Word, Incorporated.

> [18] 'You shall not take vengeance, nor bear any grudge against the sons of your people, but you shall love your neighbor as yourself; I am the LORD. (Lev. 19:18 NAU)

The idea about hating your enemy is not a direct quotation of the Hebrew Scriptures but rather a situation of necessity.

> [2] "No one of illegitimate birth shall enter the assembly of the LORD; none of his *descendants*, even to the tenth generation, shall enter the assembly of the LORD. [3] "No Ammonite or Moabite shall enter the assembly of the LORD; none of their *descendants*, even to the tenth generation, shall ever enter the assembly of the LORD, (Deut. 23:2-3 NAU)

To fully appreciate this understanding of Deuteronomy 23:2-3 is to examine why the LORD said that the Ammonite or Moabite were not welcomed into the Assembly of Israel. The reason is given in the verses that follow:

> [4] because they did not meet you with food and water on the way when you came out of Egypt, and because they hired against you Balaam the son of Beor from Pethor of Mesopotamia, to curse you. (Deut. 23:4 NAU)

Since Ruth was the great-grand mother of King David, and she was a Moabite, then the exclusion of the Moabites from the Assembly of Israel must have been lifted. Unfortunately, the hatred toward the Moabites continued. Israel and Moab battled each other for many centuries.

Phrase Study

1. Εσεσθε οὖν ὑμεῖς τέλειοι (Matt. 5:48 BYZ)

What does it mean to be perfect? (v. 48)

The understanding of "to be perfect" has been interpreted by the church in a Greek manner. The Greek abstract ideal of perfection is being untarnished by participation in the material world. For the Qumran community it meant to follow all the community's rules.[30] The translation of the Greek word τέλειος in this verse as "perfect" comes from its usage in the Septuagint.

> LXE **Deuteronomy 18:13** Thou shalt be perfect before the Lord thy God. (Deut. 18:13 LXE)

To be perfect before the LORD is to have a single-minded belief in the one and true God of Israel in all aspects of life. Therefore, the Hebraic concept of perfect, in this context, is to obey the commands and laws of the LORD without question and to the best of one's abilities. It is not to become like the LORD but rather to act like the LORD through our words and actions because the LORD follows His laws and we follow the LORD.

Greek View	Essences View	Hebraic View
Untarnished by the Material World	To follow without question the community's rules	Obey the Laws of the LORD to the best of one's ability

---

[30] The New Interpreter's Bible Commentary. Nashville: Abingdon Press, 2015.

Scripture cross references

| Verse 43 | Lev 19:18; Deu 23:3-6 |
| Verse 44 | Lev 19:18; Deu 23:3-6 |

Culture Section

[Matthew 5:43-47]

In the Torah Moses encouraged the Israelites to be friendly toward their neighbors and the strangers in their lands. Yeshua complements that by saying that we should love our enemies. The kind of love that he was referring to was that we need to be warm towards our enemies and to be kind and amicable to them. Therefore, if your enemy is hungry then you would give him bread to eat and if he is thirsty you would give him water to drink, which can be found in Proverbs 25:21. If you actualize Yeshua's concept then you have no enemies. Yeshua central theme was the practice of peace and reconciliation which leads to love. Hatred and vengeance only breeds more hatred and vengeance.

Yeshua knew that the power of love is certainly stronger than the armor of the flesh. Yeshua wanted us to apply his concept of love and not hate, for this would bring the manifestation of the kingdom of God.

The Hebrew Scripture never says, "hate your enemy." Many Christians blame Moses and the Hebrew Scriptures for the ordinance that we can hate our neighbors. But this is not a concept in the Torah. Throughout the years rabbis would put personal notes on Scripture and they developed the concept that we should love our neighbor only applied to other Israelites. Yeshua is reminding us that God's love is for all people. He is also reminding us that our neighbor is not just our own compatriots but all other people. Yeshua is reminding us that God never said, "hate your neighbor."

Near Easterners believed that their personal enemy was God's personal enemy, and as such, God's enemy deserved ruin an utter destruction. This concept can be found in several places in the Hebrew Scripture especially in Psalm 109:5 – 20. Yeshua was telling us that we must pray for those who persecute us because when we pray for people we can turn our hearts from hatred to love.

The concept of a benevolent father for all people was a new concept that Yeshua was introducing. Ancient people believed that only the righteous should prosper and the wicked should not. Yeshua taught us that God is benevolent father who blesses the good people and the bad people, the just and the unjust. Yeshua taught that God desires mercy and compassion for all people above all religious ordinances and sacrifices because God is compassionate to all people. God wants to change the wicked and unjust and rid them of their evil ways.

[Matthew 5:48 – an expansion of the definition of perfection]

The Greek word *telious* is translated into English as "perfection." Yeshua knew that none of us could ever be perfect as God is perfect. Using the Peshitta, the Aramaic Christian Scriptures, the word *gmeera* is used. This wording means "completeness, wholeness, maturity, inclusive." What Yeshua is referring to is that he wants every one of us to have a complete understanding of what God's kingdom is all about. If we understand everything there is about the kingdom of God, then we should be able to prosper and live properly in the kingdom. Therefore, for us today we should be concentrating on Bible study and learning God's word.[31]

---

[31] IBID.

Thoughts

This passage is the conclusion of the section of the Sermon on the Mount dealing with the "love your neighbor" commandment. The climax is that a person needs to become perfect, that is follow Yeshua's commandments to become a member of the Kingdom of Heaven. Regarding loving your neighbor, the lesson is that all people are one's neighbor and should be treated equally in the Kingdom of Heaven.

"Love your neighbor" is a difficult thing to do at times. One's enemy can be one's neighbor. Yeshua is saying that the treatment of an enemy should be to pray for that person(s) so that he/she will get their life straightened out and will follow the commandments of the LORD. Therefore, one must pray for one's enemies so that they will come to serve the LORD. This interpretation of Yeshua's word fits into the first century view of Judaism. This belief was expressed in the Medieval work names "The Orchot Tazaddkim.[32]"

Reflections

Are there people who should be sent to Hell on judgment day? When you reflect upon the people you knew and known throughout your life the answer is probably "yes, there are people who should be in Hell." In addition, there are probably some people you know or have known who you would like to do "something" to because of their treatment to you. As Yeshua said in the previous passage, "life's not fair." There are nasty people in the world who are doing quite well in life. Then there are people who are wonderful, caring, loving people who are poor. Again, Yeshua said that life is not always fair.

---

[32] Orchot Tzaddikim (Hebrew: ארחות צדיקים) is a book on Jewish ethics written in Germany in the 15th century, entitled Sefer ha-Middot by the author, but called Orḥot Ẓaddiḳim by a later copyist. Under this title a Yiddish translation, from which the last chapter and some other passages were omitted, was printed at Isny in 1542, although the Hebrew original did not appear until some years later (Prague, 1581). Subsequently, however, the book was frequently printed in both languages. Source: https://en.wikipedia.org/wiki/Orchot_Tzaddikim

Therefore, let's take a different approach to love your enemies. That approach which fits into Yeshua's words is that we should pray for our enemies to come into a relationship with Yeshua and that they will give up their evil ways. It is a type of evangelism that all followers and disciples of Yeshua are commanded to do. The Kingdom of Heaven was established to include all the peoples of the world. Unfortunately, in Yeshua's day, as in our day, there are numerous people who do not know God and do not follow God's commandments. So, it becomes our responsibility to pray for those people and to demonstrate to them that Yeshua's love is for them too through our words and actions. Being a part of the Kingdom of Heaven is not just a special gift from God. It is a gift to anyone who profess Yeshua as the Messiah and places their lives before God and desiring to become a part of the Kingdom of Heaven. It is then our individual job and the church's job to teach the once enemy the ways of Yeshua. It is easy to hate someone. It is difficult to love your enemy. Yeshua never took the easy road and expects us to do the same thing.

Matthew 6:1-4

Language

New American Standard 1995	Koine Greek
[1] "Beware of practicing your righteousness before men to be noticed by them; otherwise you have no reward with your Father who is in heaven. [2] "So when you give to the poor, do not sound a trumpet before you, as the hypocrites do in the synagogues and in the streets, so that they may be honored by men. Truly I say to you, they have their reward in full. [3] "But when you give to the poor, do not let your left hand know what your right hand is doing, [4] so that your giving will be in secret; and your Father who sees *what is done* in secret will reward you.	[1] Προσέχετε τὴν ἐλεημοσύνην ὑμῶν μὴ ποιεῖν ἔμπροσθεν τῶν ἀνθρώπων, πρὸς τὸ θεαθῆναι αὐτοῖς· εἰ δὲ μήγε, μισθὸν οὐκ ἔχετε παρὰ τῷ πατρὶ ὑμῶν τῷ ἐν τοῖς οὐρανοῖς. [2] Ὅταν οὖν ποιῇς ἐλεημοσύνην, μὴ σαλπίσῃς ἔμπροσθέν σου, ὥσπερ οἱ ὑποκριταὶ ποιοῦσιν ἐν ταῖς συναγωγαῖς καὶ ἐν ταῖς ῥύμαις, ὅπως δοξασθῶσιν ὑπὸ τῶν ἀνθρώπων· ἀμὴν λέγω ὑμῖν, ἀπέχουσιν τὸν μισθὸν αὐτῶν. [3] Σοῦ δὲ ποιοῦντος ἐλεημοσύνην, μὴ γνώτω ἡ ἀριστερά σου τί ποιεῖ ἡ δεξιά σου, [4] ὅπως ᾖ σου ἡ ἐλεημοσύνη ἐν τῷ κρυπτῷ· καὶ ὁ πατήρ σου ὁ βλέπων ἐν τῷ κρυπτῷ αὐτὸς ἀποδώσει σοι ἐν τῷ φανερῷ.

Process of Discovery
Linguistics Section

Linguistic Structure

A [1] "Beware of practicing your righteousness before men to be noticed by them; otherwise you have no reward with your Father who is in heaven.

> **B** [2] "So when you give to the poor,

>> **C** do not sound a trumpet before you, as the hypocrites do in the synagogues and in the streets, so that they may be honored by men. Truly I say to you, they have their reward in full.

> **B'** [3] "But when you give to the poor, do not let your left hand know what your right hand is doing,

A' [4] so that your giving will be in secret; and your Father who sees *what is done* in secret will reward you. (Matt. 6:1-4 NAU)

Discussion

This chiasm is centered on the knowledge that people who give to the poor and make it public knowledge received their reward from humankind and not from God.

Questioning the Passage

1. What righteousness is Yeshua speaking of in verse one?

   Yeshua is referring to the three types of Jewish piety. The Greek word δικαιοσύνη means righteousness. The author probably should have used the word εὐσέβεια which means piety. The three types of Jewish piety are: almsgiving, prayer and fasting.[33] Yeshua does not give a command that His followers are to follow Jewish piety. Since He was talking to an audience of mostly Jewish people, He did not have to tell them to religiously act. The people knew that they needed to show their piety before God.

---

[33] Hagner, D. A. (1998). *Matthew 1–13* (Vol. 33A, p. 139). Dallas: Word, Incorporated.

2. What does the metaphor "a trumpet" mean? (v. 2)

A trumpet was used to let people know that an announcement was about to be made. The announcement could be the beginning or end of a holy day like Rosh HaShannah or Yom Kippur. Yeshua said that when one gives to help a poor person that they must not announce it. This is tied to the practice of the hypocrite. Hypocrite in Greek means an actor in a play. It is applied to people who perform religious acts with an eye on the human grandstand.[34]

3. What does "honor by men" mean? (v. 2)

There is a trifold command by Yeshua with respect to almsgiving. Honor by men is human recognition of performing any of the three good deeds.

    1. Do not make an announcement about giving alms (trumpet)

    2. Almsgiving is not to be used for human honors (hypocrites)

    3. Give almsgiving in secret (left and know what your right hand is doing)

4. What does the expression "do not let your left hand know what your right hand is doing" mean? (v. 3)

The left hand will always know what the right had is doing. This is a metaphor saying that religious piety is a duty that is due to God and to no one else.

5. Why should giving be done in secrecy? (v. 4)

Perhaps Yeshua is telling us that there will be times that openly telling the community about an almsgiving could cause tension. Those who cannot afford to make an almsgiving or a large giving, may become jealous and that can lead to a breakdown of the community. Another possibility is that when an alms gift is announced that the

---

[34] The New Interpreter's Bible Commentary. Nashville: Abingdon Press, 2015.

audience are humans. In secrecy only, God knows about the gift. God will remember the gifts given in secrecy and will reward the giver in Heaven.

6. What is the difference between alms giving and tithing? (general question)
   Tithing is considered the portion that God takes as His. This is biblically a tithe or ten percent of one's income. Almsgiving is personal giving beyond the tithe.

Culture Section

Discussion

In Aramaic the word *zedhqatha*, which is used in verse one, is translated as "alms." The Aramaic version of the verse reads, "Beware of practicing your alms before…." This Aramaic word means "a right, a rule, a just or righteous act or proper thing to do." The emphasis of this word is an act of goodness involving the giving of money.

In Yeshua's day unjust rulers had reduced people into poverty with their excessive taxes. Many people could not pay the tax which forced them into poverty thus forcing them to seek out alms. This was an embarrassing thing to do. Many people of that day would rather starve then ask for a handout. Many times, there would be discussions about a person receiving alms in the marketplaces and synagogues.

"Let not your left hand know what your right hand is doing" is an Aramaic metaphor saying, "let no one know that you are giving alms." God knows who is giving alms and who is not. In Yeshua's day many rich people gave alms openly so that everyone in the community could see what they were doing.

Cultural Echoes

1. Giving to the poor

> [11] "For the poor will never cease *to be* in the land; therefore I command you, saying, 'You shall freely open your hand to your brother, to your needy and poor in your land.' (Deut. 15:11 NAU)

> Helping the poor of the community was very important for the community of Israel to do. "Don Isaac Abravanel, a 15th-century Spanish commentator, identifies three primary reasons for giving tzedakah: to express mercy on the poor; to recognize the poor person as your relative; and to commit to sustaining your community. With this list, Abravanel proposes a three-pronged approach to interacting with the poor."[35]

Culture and Linguistics Section

Discussion

When giving alms to a person in need is a righteous thing to do. It shows a concern for those who are less fortunate and is a sharing of one's blessings that God has bestowed. Since the recipient of the almsgiving would be ashamed, the secrecy allowed the receiver to keep some dignity. Not announcing almsgiving kept the process private. Also, since it is a righteous act the giver does it for God.

Main/Center Point

This section of Matthew's Gospel has Yeshua talking about the three aspects of Jewish piety. The first one He discusses is almsgiving. Basically, it is an important thing to do, if one can, and it must be done in secret because the audience of the act is God and not people. This idea also allows the receiver to have dignity.

---

[35] Jacobs, Jill. "Jewish Attitudes Toward Poverty." My Jewish Learning. Accessed August 01, 2018. https://www.myjewishlearning.com/article/jewish-attitudes-toward-poverty/.

Thoughts

In the church today, there are several types of offerings. The weekly offering, the tithe, is considered a giving. That is one way to view it and the church has expressed that view for centuries. Here is another, perhaps a better way to understand tithing. It is allowing God to take His portion of what He gives us to be stewards of. God gives us blessings from Heaven. Then God takes back what is His. That is the tithe. Almsgiving is what one offers to the poor after God has taken His portion. That amount is up to the giver. God's portion is defined in Scripture as a tithe, ten percent. Alms giving does not have an amount. Some will argue that if the amount of the fields that are not to be harvested or gleaned that alms giving is about twenty-five percent of one's income. The interesting discovery in this Scripture is that in Yeshua's day poor people felt ashamed to accept alms. It meant that they could not take care of themselves and their families. A family would do any kind of work necessary to earn income opposed to taking alms. Today we call almsgiving welfare and, in most countries, especially in the U.S., the government collects taxes and redistributes the wealth in the form of welfare. The problem that has developed over the decades of doing this is that many people who are receiving government welfare have decided that they are not ashamed of receiving it. In fact, most do not want to get off welfare because they get more money from the government and church handouts than they would earn at a job. Imagine what the U.S. would look like if its people on welfare and government handout would feel ashamed to receive the help and would go to work. A part of the welfare system should be a program to get people off it.

Reflections

Many churches are full of people who like to give alms but demand the recognition that they have given. In a church there were three wealthy families. If each family allowed God to take His portion back (ten percent) then the church would never have any financial problems. But that did not happen. Why? Probably because allowing God to take back His portion is not something that is advertised. When this church needed an elevator, a new roof, new carpets in the huge sanctuary, one of the three families would jump in to pay the bill. After the bill was paid they demanded that a plaque be put on the wall, so that everyone in the church could see who paid the bill. This is an example of boasting about alms giving and is in direct contradiction to what Yeshua says about almsgiving. Plaques and bookplates are examples of telling the congregation who was the almsgiver of that item. To thank a person(s) for a gift to the church is fine. However, when it is made into a plaque that becomes a permanent fixture, is not fine. The other behavior that occurs is when the almsgiver decides that their gift to the church, must be a material item, comes under their control for life. An example is that at a church some trees were being planted. The cost was approximate $3,500. One member stood up in church on a Sunday and offered to pay for the trees. That was wonderful except that she began to be critical about how the trees were attended to and made demands of the pastor to have the trees treated in a specific way. Almsgiving ownership in the church is a church killer. Things cannot be changed or updated unless the original giver says so. It may be good for church to abolish all recognition plagues and concentrate on the Words of the Lord Yeshua.

Matthew 6-5-15

Language

New American Standard 1995	Koine Greek
5 "When you pray, you are not to be like the hypocrites; for they love to stand and pray in the synagogues and on the street corners so that they may be seen by men. Truly I say to you, they have their reward in full.	5 Καὶ ὅταν προσεύχῃ, οὐκ ἔσῃ ὥσπερ οἱ ὑποκριταί, ὅτι φιλοῦσιν ἐν ταῖς συναγωγαῖς καὶ ἐν ταῖς γωνίαις τῶν πλατειῶν ἑστῶτες προσεύχεσθαι, ὅπως ἂν φανῶσιν τοῖς ἀνθρώποις· ἀμὴν λέγω ὑμῖν ὅτι ἀπέχουσιν τὸν μισθὸν αὐτῶν.
6 "But you, when you pray, go into your inner room, close your door and pray to your Father who is in secret, and your Father who sees *what is done* in secret will reward you.	6 Σὺ δέ, ὅταν προσεύχῃ, εἴσελθε εἰς τὸ ταμιεῖόν σου, καὶ κλείσας τὴν θύραν σου, πρόσευξαι τῷ πατρί σου τῷ ἐν τῷ κρυπτῷ· καὶ ὁ πατήρ σου ὁ βλέπων ἐν τῷ κρυπτῷ ἀποδώσει σοι ἐν τῷ φανερῷ.
7 "And when you are praying, do not use meaningless repetition as the Gentiles do, for they suppose that they will be heard for their many words.	7 Προσευχόμενοι δὲ μὴ βαττολογήσητε, ὥσπερ οἱ ἐθνικοί· δοκοῦσιν γὰρ ὅτι ἐν τῇ πολυλογίᾳ αὐτῶν εἰσακουσθήσονται.
8 "So do not be like them; for your Father knows what you need before you ask Him.	8 Μὴ οὖν ὁμοιωθῆτε αὐτοῖς· οἶδεν γὰρ ὁ πατὴρ ὑμῶν ὧν χρείαν ἔχετε, πρὸ τοῦ ὑμᾶς αἰτῆσαι αὐτόν.
9 "Pray, then, in this way: 'Our Father who is in heaven, Hallowed be Your name.	9 Οὕτως οὖν προσεύχεσθε ὑμεῖς· Πάτερ ἡμῶν ὁ ἐν τοῖς οὐρανοῖς, ἁγιασθήτω τὸ ὄνομά σου.
10 'Your kingdom come. Your will be done, on earth as it is in heaven.	10 Ἐλθέτω ἡ βασιλεία σου. Γενηθήτω τὸ θέλημά σου, ὡς ἐν οὐρανῷ, καὶ ἐπὶ τῆς γῆς.
11 'Give us this day our daily bread.	11 Τὸν ἄρτον ἡμῶν τὸν ἐπιούσιον δὸς ἡμῖν σήμερον.
12 'And forgive us our debts, as we also have forgiven our debtors.	12 Καὶ ἄφες ἡμῖν τὰ ὀφειλήματα ἡμῶν, ὡς καὶ ἡμεῖς ἀφίεμεν τοῖς ὀφειλέταις ἡμῶν.
13 'And do not lead us into temptation, but deliver us from evil. *For Yours is the kingdom and the power and the glory forever. Amen .'*	13 Καὶ μὴ εἰσενέγκῃς ἡμᾶς εἰς πειρασμόν, ἀλλὰ ῥῦσαι ἡμᾶς ἀπὸ τοῦ πονηροῦ. Ὅτι σοῦ ἐστιν ἡ βασιλεία καὶ ἡ δύναμις καὶ ἡ δόξα εἰς τοὺς αἰῶνας. Ἀμήν.
	14 Ἐὰν γὰρ ἀφῆτε τοῖς ἀνθρώποις τὰ παραπτώματα αὐτῶν, ἀφήσει καὶ ὑμῖν ὁ πατὴρ ὑμῶν ὁ οὐράνιος·

<table>
<tr>
<td>14 "For if you forgive others for their transgressions, your heavenly Father will also forgive you.
15 "But if you do not forgive others, then your Father will not forgive your transgressions.</td>
<td>15 ἐὰν δὲ μὴ ἀφῆτε τοῖς ἀνθρώποις τὰ παραπτώματα αὐτῶν, οὐδὲ ὁ πατὴρ ὑμῶν ἀφήσει τὰ παραπτώματα ὑμῶν.</td>
</tr>
</table>

Process of Discovery

Linguistics Section

Linguistic Structure

A [5] "When you pray, you are not to be like the hypocrites; for they love to stand and pray in the synagogues and on the street corners so that they may be seen by men. Truly I say to you, they have their reward in full.

> **B** [6] "But you, when you pray, go into your inner room, close your door and pray to your Father who is in secret, and your Father who sees *what is done* in secret will reward you.

A' [7] "And when you are praying, do not use meaningless repetition as the Gentiles do, for they suppose that they will be heard for their many words.

> **B'** [8] "So do not be like them; for your Father knows what you need before you ask Him.

[Lord's Prayer] [9] "Pray, then, in this way: 'Our Father who is in heaven, Hallowed be Your name. [10] 'Your kingdom come. Your will be done, on earth as it is in heaven. [11] 'Give us this day our daily bread. [12] 'And forgive us our debts, as we also have forgiven our debtors. [13] 'And do not lead us into temptation, but deliver us from evil. *For Yours is the kingdom and the power and the glory forever. Amen* .' [14] "For if you forgive others for their transgressions, your heavenly Father will also forgive you. [15] "But if you do not forgive others, then your Father will not forgive your transgressions.

Discussion

The first part of the passage is an A-B-A'-B' chiasm created by the imperative "when you pray." Verses 9 to 15 is the Lord's Prayer. This is not the complete Lord's Prayer that is spoken in churches today. Over the centuries the church determined to add extra lines to it.

Questioning the Passage

1. What is the reward Jesus mentions in verse five?

    The reward are treasures in the world to come.

2. What was the inner room? (v. 6)

    Most Near Easterner homes had a small adjoining room to the house which was called the "inner room." In this room the family kept their valuables and supplies, so that they would be protected from robbers. A small door was inside the home which would allow access to the inner room. Houses were quite small with multi-generations of family members living in them. Privacy was something of a premium. However, in the inner room one could find some moments of privacy. Many people liked to pray in the market places, so that people could witness the event. In the market place shop owners would kneel on a cloak and pray when there were no customers in the shop. They would mumble their prayers, so that people knew that they were praying but did not know what the prayers were about. Jesus did not like this kind of public prayer; thus, he told His disciples not to engage anytime in public prayer. People who wanted to ensure that other people would see them praying would find a conspicuous place in public to pray.

Semites believed that God was a spirit that mortal eyes cannot see God. God became localized over the centuries and it was believed that God could only be communicated with at Jerusalem (the Temple), the synagogues and other high places. Today Semites believe that God is everywhere. Jesus could have also been communicating the concept of God being everything and not just in Jerusalem.[36]

3. What are the components of the Lord's Prayer?[37]

Abba (Father) - God is a divine parent and Jesus says that one can approach God in the same manner that a child can approach a loving father. God only wants the best for His children. Abba is an endearing and affectionate expression. Family tradition were very important to the Hebrews of Jesus's day. Bringing God into the family shows trust, and respect for God.

Daily Bread – this refers not only to bread but to the daily food supplies necessary for life. People in Jesus's day feared a lack of food. A drought would cause many people to perish. The Roman armies occupying Judea and the Galilee put a heavy strain on an already strained food chain. It is not that the people of Jesus's day did not believe that God would feed them, rather they were concerned about greed, hoarding and other conflicts that arise when food supplies are short. The people were praying that these internal conflicts would not occur.

Canceling debts – this verse can be about actual debts and it can be translated as offenses. In the Aramaic language "debts" is a metaphor for "sin" in the Lord's prayer. Forgiveness is at the heart of Jesus's ministry. Therefore, it would be logical that He

---

[36] Errico, Rocco A., and George M. Lamsa. Aramaic Light on the Gospel of Matthew: A Commentary on the Teachings of Jesus from the Aramaic and Unchanged Near Eastern Customs. Santa Fe, NM: Noohra Foundation, 2000.
[37] IBID.

would add it to the general prayer. Forgiving others is a first step to one own's forgiveness.

Lead us not into temptation – this verse is problematic because it is saying that God could lead us into temptation. The Aramaic text reads: "And do not let us enter into temptation." This translation is more in line with what Jesus and the Hebrew Scriptures teach. It is easy to fall into temptation. Evil is everywhere, therefore praying for protection from evil is logical.

Scripture cross references

Verse 6   Isa 26:20

Culture Section

Discussion

One complication with the understanding of the Lord's prayer comes from it being written in Greek, a language that Jesus did not speak, and its being westernized and brought into the Mithras cult when Paul was converting the Mithras House churches into Jesus house churches. It is questionable as to whether the disciples needed Jesus to teach them how to pray. The Mithras churches after having been converted would have wanted to learn how to address their new God. Also, several of the Mithras prayers and liturgies did not fit the Christian ethics that Paul left with the new churches. Therefore, it is possible that they wanted to learn how to please Jesus by praying in the manner that Jesus wanted. That would attest as to why Matthew's Gospel needed a section on how to pray.

Going under the premise that Jesus was asked about prayer, his response, in Aramaic, would look a bit different in English. The following translation considers the Aramaic version of the New Testament, the Peshitta, and includes the cultural aspects.[38]

Our Father who is everywhere,

Let Your Name be set apart.

Come Your Kingdom (Your counsel)

Let Your desire be, as in the universe, also on the earth.

Provide us our needful bread from day to day.

And free us from our offenses, as also we have freed our offenders.

And do not let us enter into temptation but separate us from error.

For belongs to You, the Kingdom, the power, and the song and praises.

From all ages throughout all ages.

Sealed trust, and faithfulness.

Questioning the passage

1. How did the people in Jesus's day view prayer?

   Prayer was viewed as a vehicle which prepared one to express needs to God and to offer thanksgiving for blessings received, so that one would be qualified to receive what God was providing. Prayer was also a way to trap the voice of God. This meant to offer prayer in silence just listening to hear God's direction for one's life. The root word for prayer means "to trap."[39] One becomes aware of God in prayer and can hear His presence. The difficult part is to silence one's mind to hear God.

---

[38] Errico, Rocco A. Setting a Trap for God: The Aramaic Prayer of Jesus. Unity Village, MO: Unity Books, 1997.
[39] Errico, Rocco A., and George M. Lamsa. Aramaic Light on the Gospel of Matthew: A Commentary on the Teachings of Jesus from the Aramaic and Unchanged Near Eastern Customs. Santa Fe, NM: Noohra Foundation, 2000.

2. What did people think prayer accomplished in Jesus' day?

   Since God knows what we need, why pray for anything? The misconception of prayer today is that prayer can change God. Prayer does not change God but rather it changes us! Prayer helps us to understand ourselves. Prayer can attune us to the spiritual forces that surrounds us and are in us. Our spirits can be nourished by prayer.[40] Ancient people envisioned prayer as a communication method to speak to God. Essentially prayer allows a person to realign themselves to God and to open the communications pathway, thus hearing God's voice and feeling His presence.

3. Could there be another reason for the development of the Lord's prayer that occurred long after Jesus's life?

   Blessing 12 of the Amidah says: "Heretics" - May there be no hope for apostates, and may You quickly uproot the insolent reign in our day, and may the Christians and heretics instantly perish. May they be erased from the book of life, and may they not be written with the righteous. Blessed are You, Adonai, who humbles the insolent.

   Gamaliel introduced the Amidah sometime between 60 and 70 CE (perhaps even earlier) and so if this timeline is used combined with blessing 12, which is a direct assault on the Jews who followed Jesus the Messiah, there would be a reason for the church to repudiate blessing 12.

   The Christians got their name as follows:

   > So, for a whole year Barnabas and Saul met with the church and taught great numbers of people. The disciples were called Christians first at Antioch. (Act 11:26 NIV)

---

[40] IBID.

Paul/Saul was originally a part of the group who was trying to derail the Jesus movement.

> [NIV] Acts 9:1 Meanwhile, Saul was still breathing out murderous threats against the Lord's disciples. He went to the high priest [2] and asked him for letters to the synagogues in Damascus, so that if he found any there who belonged to the Way, whether men or women, he might take them as prisoners to Jerusalem. (Act 9:1-2 NIV)

Paul was a student of Gamaliel, so he would have known that Gamaliel was putting together the Amidah. Gamaliel believed that Jews needed a "way to pray" that would become a major part of their lives. Devote Jews have been reciting the Amidah since the day it was introduced. So, it is possible that Paul introduced the "Lord's Prayer" as he established churches. His churches started with mainly Jews, so it would be prudent to have established prayers. Jews had established prayers for so many different things already. Would not Paul "adjust" those prayers so that Jesus became a larger part of prayers?

> [3] "I am a Jew, born in Tarsus of Cilicia, but brought up in this city. I studied under Gamaliel and was thoroughly trained in the law of our ancestors. I was just as zealous for God as any of you are today. (Act 22:3 NIV)

When Matthew's Gospel was written, the Lord's Prayer would have been a part of the church moving it toward a traditional status. So, who gave us the prayer? Jesus did as far as the people remembered but was it Jesus or Paul who said Jesus gave us this prayer? Paul probably used Jesus's name more than once to bolster his convictions.

The text of the Amidah is offered so that the reader can make a comparison. The piety of traditional Jews verses the newly formed Christian sect toward prayer would indicate that the Christians liked short prayers.

The Amidah

Opening Meditation

Adonai, open my lips, that my mouth may declare your praise.

Blessing 1— Avot: "Ancestors" - Blessed are You, Adonai, our God and our ancestors' God, Abraham's God, Isaac's God, and Jacob's God, great, mighty, and revered God, supreme God, master of heaven and earth, our protector and our ancestors' protector, our security in every generation. Blessed are You, Adonai, Abraham's protector.

Blessing 2— G'vurot: "God's Power" - You are mighty, you humble the proud, you are strong, you judge the wicked, and you live forever; You support the dead, cause the wind to blow and bring down the dew, and sustain life giving life to the dead; in the blink of an eye you bring salvation. Blessed are you, Adonai, who gives life to the dead.

Blessing 3 - K'dushat Hashem: "Sanctification of God's Name" - Holy are You, and your name is revered; there is no god other than You. Blessed are You, Adonai, the holy God.

Blessing 4— Binah: "Knowledge" - Favor us, with your knowledge, our father, and with your Torah's understanding and wisdom. Blessed are you, Adonai, who favors people with knowledge.

Blessing 5— T'shuvah: "Repentance" - Bring us back to You, Adonai, that we shall return. Renew our days as of old. Blessed are You, Adonai, who takes pleasure in repentance.

Blessing 6— S'lichah: "Forgiveness" - Forgive us, our father, for we have sinned before You; wipe out and remove our transgressions from before your eyes, for great is your mercy. Blessed are You, Adonai, who is quick to forgive.

Blessing 7— G'ulah: "Deliverance" - See our affliction and fight our fight; redeem us for the sake of your name. Blessed are You, Adonai, who redeems Israel.

Blessing 8— R'fu'ah: "Healing" - Heal us, Adonai, from the pains of our heart, and remove sorrow and complaint from among us. Bring healing to our wounds. Blessed are You, Adonai, who heals the sick among his people Israel.

Blessing 9— Shanim: "Years" - Bless this year for us for goodness through its produce, Adonai our God, and quickly bring the year near that ends our exile. Grant dew and rain on the surface of the ground, and eternal abundance from the stores of your goodness, and grant blessing through the work of our hands. Blessed are You, Adonai, who blesses our years.

Blessing 10— Kibbutz G'luyot: "Gathering the Exiles" - Sound a great shofar for our freedom, and lift a banner for the gathering of our exiles. Blessed are You, Adonai, who gathers the dispersed among his people Israel.

Blessing 11— Mishpat: "Justice" - Restore our judges as in days of old, and our counselors as in former times, and reign over us, You alone. Blessed are You, Adonai, who loves justice.

Blessing 12— Minim: "Heretics" - May there be no hope for apostates, and may You quickly uproot the insolent reign in our day, and may the Christians and heretics instantly perish. May they be erased from the book of life, and may they not be written with the righteous. Blessed are You, Adonai, who humbles the insolent.

Blessing 13— Tsadikim: "The Righteous" - Show compassion to righteous converts, and give us a good reward with those who do your will. Blessed are You, Adonai, who is the trust of the righteous.

Blessing 14— Y'rushalayim v'david: "Jerusalem and David" - Have mercy, Adonai our God, in your great mercy, on Israel your people, and on Jerusalem your city, and on Zion where your presence dwells, and on your palace and on your habitation and on your righteous servant David's kingdom. Blessed are You, Adonai, David's God, who builds Jerusalem.

Blessing 15— T'fillah: "Prayer" - Adonai our God, hear the voice of our prayers and have mercy on us, for You are the God who is gracious and merciful. Blessed are You, Adonai, who hears prayer.

Blessings 16 to 18: Blessings of Thanksgiving

Blessing 16— Avodah: "Sacrificial Service" - Find favor, Adonai our God, and dwell in Zion that You may be served by your servants in Jerusalem. Blessed are You, Adonai, whom we will serve with awe.

Blessing 17— Hoda'ah: "Grateful Acknowledgment" - We gratefully acknowledge You— You are Adonai our God and our ancestors' God—for all the goodness, the kindness, and the mercy that you have shown and done for us and for our ancestors before us, and if we say our step has faltered, your kindness will support us. Blessed are You, whom is it good to gratefully acknowledge.

Blessing 18— Birkat Kohanim: "The Priestly Blessing" - Grant your peace on Israel your people and on your city and on your heritage, and bless all of us as one. Blessed are you, Adonai, who brings peace.

Closing Meditation

May the words of my mouth and the thoughts of my heart be favorable before You, Adonai, my rock and my redeemer.

Zohar

The Zohar[i] tells us that a person is made of three distinct components – the *nefesh* (flesh), the *ruach* (the soul/spirit), and the *neshamah* (the spark of God). The first component is the flesh. The flesh is the biological body of a person. The biological body is created through the act of reproduction. The second component comes from the heavenly realm and that is the soul (or spirit) of the individual. Before our soul's come to earth we reside in the lower waters of Heaven. The soul is made up of two parts, a male part and a female part. The two remain together from its creation until it moves into the Sefirah[ii] Yesod[iii]. The soul splits into two parts, male and female, when it enters the Sefirah of Malchut (the material realm) and enters a created flesh. Also, the combined male and female soul is also referred to as two souls connected to each other. Then during one's life the two soul-mates attempt to find each other on Earth. If that does not happen then when both souls return to Yesod, upon death, they reconnect. The third component is the spark of God that resides in each of us which makes us aware of our surroundings, our life and that we are a part of God. This is the likeness of God in each of us, which is this spark, which is explained in Genesis 1:27.

> 27 God created man in His own image, in the image of God He created him; male and female He created them. (Gen. 1:27 NAU)

The spark of God in us is what enables us to talk with God. We reside in the material world while God resides in the spiritual world. The idea that God can hear our prayers and that we can hear God's voice is called mysticism. The Zohar is one of the major writings of Hebraic Mysticism. Thus, the mystical connection between the physical world and the spiritual world is accomplished by the spark of God in each of us.

Prayer can be envisioned as conduits and pathways from Malchut to Yesod and then to the rest of the Sefirot in the Tree of Life. The following chart is the author's interpretation of how prayer works within the Tree of Life.

The Shekinah[iv] of God is a part of the prayer cycle. The Shekinah responds to the need for bodily healing. Healing best occurs when the individual in need of healing is praying for him/herself with other people are praying. The power of prayer is transformed when it rises to Yeshod, the lower waters of Heaven, and is accumulated with the prayer power of others and then it is sent to the Shekinah for healing.

One question is how can our prayers be effective in Malchut when God is in the spiritual world? Prayers for material gains, like money, cars, house, and so forth are prayers that will not be answered. God answers spiritual prayers and healing concerns. How can this occur? The "transformation" point is the spark of God that is in each of us. Our prayers can travel from our souls to Yesod through the spark of God that is within us. That spark is spiritual as the Shekinah resides in Malchut, so does the neshamah. Our prayers are transformed into spiritual power which leaves Malchut and enters Yesod through the spark of God in us.

But healing is of the physical flesh. The power of healing is transmitted to us through the Shekinah. The Shekinah is a spiritual force of God which resides in Malchut but can "communicate" with God through the connection between Yesod and Malchut. The spark of God within us can receive the healing forces and if possible cause healing to occur. When the force of healing is within a person it will be effective if the person is also praying for healing, thus becoming receptive. It must be understood that there are situations where healing cannot help. For example, damaged heart muscles cannot be regenerated. All the praying in the world will not change that biological fact. The rules of our flesh can prevent certain healing from occurring. There is scientific proof that prayer for healing causes a person to have a positive attitude and that a positive attitude will assist the body's immune system to bring healing.

So, our communication pathway to God is the spark of God which resides in each of us. Our prayer request enters Heaven through Yesod and travels to Tiferet. In the realm of Tiferet the prayer request is sent to the Sefirah which can answer the prayer. The following chart is the author's interpretation of the prayer pathways. In the Zohar the prayer pathways can be found in what is called the Chamber of Abba and Imma.[v]

Mystical Methodology to Prayer

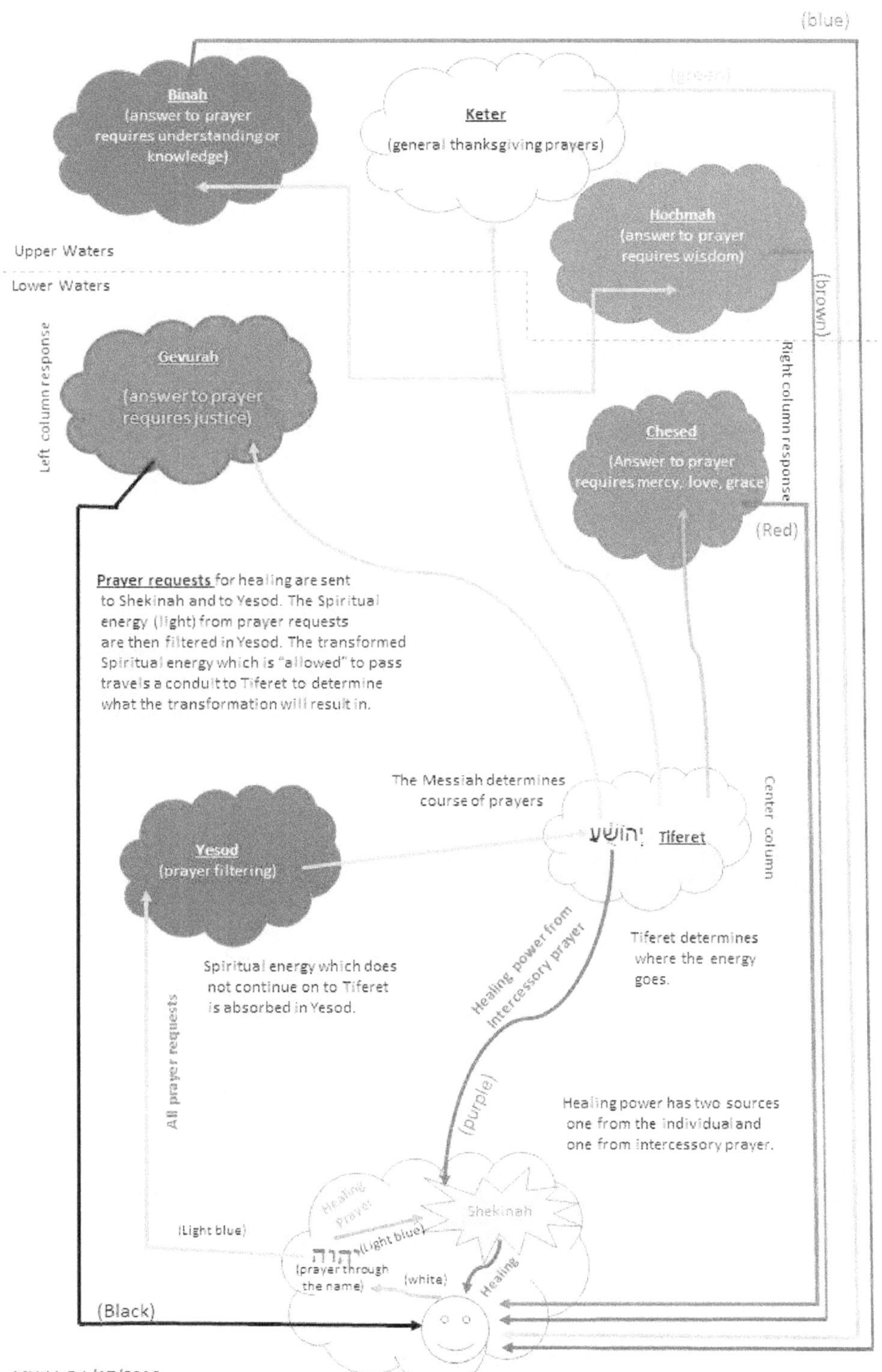

Additional Information - Tzeruf Meditation/Prayer

"Tzeruf is a 4700 old meditation. The technique in the Bible is labeled as "calling in the name of the Lord." This meditation focuses on using the true name of God. It contains the Hebrew alphabet meanings and their mystical properties. The levels of the soul are discussed, as well as the creating of a vessel to receive the spiritual influx, how to prepare to be more spiritually and mentally receptive. This book describes in detail the instructions on how to perform vocal meditations and provides numerous meditation tables and Psalms specifically geared to produce higher states of consciousness. The sages of old have stated that these techniques can be dangerous. It has been known to go as far as making some of those who misuse the meditations to go insane."[41]

This methodology is shown on the "Mystical Methodology to Prayer" chart. The technique shown is to offer prayers through the one name of God. This is the name that Moses received on Mount Sinai and was never to be spoken except by the High Priest while he was in the inner room of the Temple at Jerusalem on the day of Yom Kippur. The pronunciation of the name of God has been lost. However, one can pray through the name. Before offering a prayer image, in your mind, the name of God in Hebrew. See the four letters. Then envision your prayers flowing through the name of God. This will act as a "filter" allowing the prayers which can be answered to rise to Heaven.

Beware that using this method can generate interesting and sometimes frightful dreams. These dreams will stop over a short period of time. If done regularly this technique will tune the mind into being able to hear the voice of God.

---

[41] "Tzeruf Basics: A Kabbalah Meditation: Dr Daniel A Elias: 9780979282607: Amazon.com: Books." Amazon. Accessed August 16, 2018. https://www.amazon.com/Tzeruf-Basics-Meditation-Daniel-Elias/dp/0979282608/ref=sr_1_2?s=books.

When you pray through the name of God you are actually praying through the neshamah, the spark of God in you. The neshamah is the "transceiver" for prayer. It is a part of the spiritual kingdom of God inside you. Communications with God are bidirectional and occur through the neshamah.

Thoughts

Why would a people who lived in faith to God must be taught how to pray? The general prayers of thanksgiving had been developed and passed down through the generations. Therefore, Jesus would not have to teach His disciples how to construct and offer prayer. However, during Jesus's day there were people who decided to offer prayer in public with the purpose of making themselves look more pious and righteous. Viewing this passage about prayer as addressing the problem, its solution is evident. Certain persons were using the gift of prayer to honor themselves before men. This would be a connection to the previous passage about almsgiving. In the previous passage Jesus warned people about using the pious act of helping others to receive the "honor of men" when indeed one should seek the "honor of God." Prayer was being used in the same manner as almsgiving, to gain honor from people. That practice is unacceptable to God and Jesus insured that His follows and disciples understood that. It also means that walking around saying "I am better than you because I follow Jesus" is another form of trying to gain the honor of men. Doing pious acts for God is because one wants to please God and nothing more. Pray in secret so that only you and God know what you are praying for. Do not pray to God so others will think more highly of you or to show you honor! What Jesus is telling us that the Hebraic pieties of almsgiving, prayer and fasting must not be corrupted by the society's culture.

Reflections

The Lord's prayer has been a part of Christian worship for centuries. In the Medieval times the last sentence about the kingdom and glory was added to the prayer. Today it is a prayer that all truly faithful Christians know. Even a person with extreme dementia can usually recite the Lord's prayer if you start it for them. It is ingrained in the DNA of the church. However, that is not what Jesus wanted. He was asked how to formulate prayers. Jesus gave us the construction of prayers and expects us to use His formulation for our prayers.

1. Acknowledge God as the sovereign of the Universe who is spiritual because He resides in Heaven.

2. The name of God is a sacred word and is not be said especially in any kind of disrespect to God.

3. The desire for God's will to be done is the heart of prayer. A large part of prayer is listening for God's voice speaking.

4. Asking God to help us eliminate any petty disputes between people allows the community, the family of God to grow and flourish.

5. Who wants to enter temptation which can lead to sin? As evil inclination continues to attack the disciples of Jesus, a defense mechanism is useful.

6. Then the conclusion of the pray is another acknowledgment of the power and might of God.

In conclusion, the Lord's prayer was probably never intended to be something that we repeat every day. It is the guide to form one's own prayer and praise to God.

Effectiveness to Prayer

People pray for all kinds of things. An area to examine is prayers for material items, such as money, a car, a house, etc. God does not operate in the material world, rather God works in the spiritual world. Therefore, prayers for material objects are not effective prayers and prayers that are not going to be answered. There are times when a person prays for a material event or object and that event occurs. Is it God who intervened or was it that the prayer changed the person? Since prayer changes us and not God it seems logical to say that the prayer changed the person. Another example is prayer for a new job. Since God does not work in the material world He cannot help a person to find a new job. The prayer changes the person and makes the person more receptive to an employment opportunity that was once missed or perhaps gives the person more confidence on the next job interview.

God has given people the ability to make decisions and to determine how they will live in the material world. The Torah is the guidebook of life and Jesus's interpretations of the Torah are the ultimate guide to pleasing God. But today many persons rely on the power of prayer in areas that prayer will not make a difference. It can become an easy crutch and a way to place blame on God, instead of oneself, when the prayer is not answered. The church's theological response is if the prayer is not answered then God did not want it to happen. Perhaps the answer should be an exploration of what the prayer was asking for and determining whether it is a prayer that God could answer.

For example, a church congregation was determining whether to build an addition which would be used as a community and recreation center. So, as all good churches do the congregation entered into prayer. God does not operate in the material world. Therefore, God would not answer this prayer. However, 85% of the congregation believed that God said build the building and 15% insisted that God was saying no. Who was hearing God correctly?

Where do you find the answer to material prayers if not from God? The answer is in the Scripture. Should the church build the addition? The Scripture says that the church is to make disciples for Jesus Christ. Therefore, the question should be "does the addition help the church to make disciples for Jesus Christ?" In this case the answer was "yes." Therefore, the building was built. Prayer was not the answer. Bible study was the way to get the answer to the question. The answer was found in the Word of God. Material prayers should not be offered but rather the Scripture must be used for the answer.

If a materialistic prayer can be offered as a spiritual prayer then God might answer it. For example, I had a house to sell when I entered Christ's ministry. 9/11/01 occurred and the housing market grinded to a halt. I prayed to God to help me sell the house. I did not have the income after leaving my full-time business job to go to Seminary to afford the house. Three months passed and nothing was happening. Then I turned the prayer from "God sell the House" to "God send me a family who can learn about you as I learned about you in this house." Within two weeks the house was sold to a couple who was starting a family. The material object was the result but for God it was a spiritual oriented prayer that was answered.

There are times when prayers for healing seem to have little to no effect. Did God ignore the prayers? There are a lot of answers to this question. The answer could be as simple as God does answer a healing prayer. However, if the person is beyond physical healing it could be better for God to end the person's suffering. For example, a stage five cancer could be difficult for the body to heal. Prayer for healing gives a boost to the immune system. But is that boost enough to heal the person. Probably not at the final stage of cancer. Our physical body can heal itself. But there are body breakdowns that the body cannot heal.

Accepted prayer is converted into spiritual energy and is then returned through the Holy Spirit (the Shekinah) back to the people. It is a cycle that God created when the universe was established. To get fully in tune with God it is important to understand that this cycle exists and that one should take full advantage of it. Effective prayers are prayers for spiritual activity or bodily healing. The spiritual energy increases as the number of persons offer the same prayer. Jesus told us to be in worship as a community because when two or more pray together it magnifies the spiritual energy that God will return. Also, the individual who is a recipient of the prayer will feel the Holy Spirit when the person also prays for the same result.

Matthew 6:16-18

Language

New American Standard 1995	Koine Greek
[16] "Whenever you fast, do not put on a gloomy face as the hypocrites *do*, for they neglect their appearance so that they will be noticed by men when they are fasting. Truly I say to you, they have their reward in full. [17] "But you, when you fast, anoint your head and wash your face [18] so that your fasting will not be noticed by men, but by your Father who is in secret; and your Father who sees *what is done* in secret will reward you.	[16] Ὅταν δὲ νηστεύητε, μὴ γίνεσθε ὥσπερ οἱ ὑποκριταὶ σκυθρωποί ἀφανίζουσι γὰρ τὰ πρόσωπα αὐτῶν ὅπως φανῶσι τοῖς ἀνθρώποις νηστεύοντες ἀμὴν λέγω ὑμῖν ὅτι ἀπέχουσι τὸν μισθὸν αὐτῶν. [17] σὺ δὲ νηστεύων ἄλειψαί σου τὴν κεφαλὴν καὶ τὸ πρόσωπόν σου νίψαι, [18] ὅπως μὴ φανῇς τοῖς ἀνθρώποις νηστεύων, ἀλλὰ τῷ πατρί σου τῷ ἐν τῷ κρυπτῷ, καὶ ὁ πατήρ σου ὁ βλέπων ἐν τῷ κρυπτῷ ἀποδώσει σοι.

Process of Discovery

Linguistics Section

Linguistic Structure

[Statement] [16] "Whenever you fast, do not put on a gloomy face as the hypocrites *do*, for they neglect their appearance so that they will be noticed by men when they are fasting. Truly I say to you, they have their reward in full.

[antithetical] [17] "But you, when you fast, anoint your head and wash your face [18] so that your fasting will not be noticed by men, but by your Father who is in secret; and your Father who sees *what is done* in secret will reward you.

Discussion

Verses 17 and 18 are the opposite of what Yeshua says in verse 16. In verse 16 Yeshua is stating what was happening in His day. Verses 17 and 18 tells us what should be done.

Questioning the Passage

1. What was the general purpose of fasting?

   Today's definition is that fasting is the abstaining from food in order to humble oneself before God. In ancient times it had a different purpose.

   Fasting after the death of Saul and his sons: [13] They took their bones and buried them under the tamarisk tree at Jabesh, and fasted seven days. (1 Sam. 31:13 NAU) and [2] They mourned and wept and fasted until evening for Saul and his son Jonathan and for the people of the LORD and the house of Israel, because they had fallen by the sword. (2 Sam. 1:12 NAU)

   As a sign of penitence: [6] They gathered to Mizpah, and drew water and poured it out before the LORD, and fasted on that day and said there, "We have sinned against the LORD." And Samuel judged the sons of Israel at Mizpah. (1 Sam. 7:6 NAU)

   As an accompaniment to prayer: [16] David therefore inquired of God for the child; and David fasted and went and lay all night on the ground. [17] The elders of his household stood beside him to raise him up from the ground, but he was unwilling and would not eat food with them. (2 Sam. 12:16-17 NAU)

   To prepare oneself for divine revelation: [28] So he was there with the LORD forty days and forty nights; he did not eat bread or drink water. And he wrote on the tablets the words of the covenant, the Ten Commandments. (Exod. 34:28 NAU)

"Mosaic law prescribed fasting only in connection with observance of the Day of Atonement (Lev. 16:29–31; 23:27); otherwise, fast days were voluntary, with the exception of fasts proclaimed in times of national emergency (Judg. 20:26; 2 Chr. 20:3; Joel 2:15; 1 Macc. 3:47). The national trauma which resulted from the destruction of Jerusalem and the Exile which followed prompted regular fasts in observance of these events (Zech. 7:3, 5; 8:19). The length of a fast might be one day (2 Sam. 3:35) or night (Dan. 6:18) or as many as three (Esth. 4:16), seven (1 Sam. 31:13), or forty days (1 Kgs. 19:8)."[42]

2. When was fasting required?

Mosaic law required fasting only on Yom Kippur, the Day of Atonement.

3. What was the fasting practice of the early church?

"In the early Church fasting was observed as a preparation for important decisions (e.g., Acts 13:2–3; 14:23). Weekly fasts became a regular practice (Did. 8:1, Wednesday and Friday)."[43]

Didache 8: 1 Let not your fasts be with the hypocrites, for they fast on Mondays and Thursdays, but do you fast on Wednesdays and Fridays.

There is no reason for fasting offered in the Didache.

4. What was the Greek-Roman view of fasting?

"Basically, there are two kinds of purposes or objectives for fasting. Men fast for either spiritual or physical reasons, and both are equally valid. Spiritually, fasting

---

[42] Myers, A. C. (1987). In *The Eerdmans Bible dictionary* (p. 377). Grand Rapids, MI: Eerdmans.
[43] IBID.

helps us transcend our addiction and attachment to food, and to realize that man doesn't live by bread alone. The mind gets clearer, and spiritual awareness deepens. Freed from having to satisfy physical hunger, one can then turn one's attention to feeding the mind and spirit. Spiritual masters like Pythagoras wouldn't admit any disciple into their higher teachings unless they had first purified themselves through fasting."[44]

5. What did Yeshua say about fasting?

Yeshua being counter cultural said that looking gloomy, that is not washing, not combing the hair, wearing sack cloths and ashes should not be done when one was doing a voluntary fast. The practice of doing these extra things while fasting was a way to showoff and impress people, thus receiving the honor of men. If a person is fasting it should be done without visible signs because the fasting should be for God and not to impress people. Yeshua tells us that God will take note of the piety offered through fasting and a proper reward will to give to those who behave in this manner.

Scripture cross references

Verse 16   Isa 58:5

Culture Section

Discussion

Yeshua's discussion about fasting is considered a prescribed period of abstaining from food for a period of time. During a period of fasting sackcloth was worn. Ashes were placed on the head. The person fasting also did not wash their body. The designated days

---

[44] cristi.albu@gmail.com. "FASTING AND PURIFICATION." Greek Medicine: EGYPTIAN ROOTS, Accessed October 10, 2018. www.greekmedicine.net/hygiene/Fasting_and_Purification.html.

for voluntary fasting was Mondays and Thursdays. The Didache 8:1 calls the Hebrews hypocrites and tells the early church members not to voluntarily fast on Monday and Thursday but rather on Wednesday and Friday. The church did this to further separate itself from its Hebraic roots. In addition, the church changed the meaning of fasting to become a spiritual event as it is viewed as today.

The required Hebraic fasting day was Yom Kippur, the Day of Atonement. Later on, Jewish tradition called for public fasting on Rosh Ha-Shannah, New Year's Day, and the Ninth of Ab, the lamentation of the destruction of Jerusalem and the Temple by the Babylonian army in 586 BCE and by the Roman Emperor Titus in 70 CE. Hebrews could voluntarily fast as a sign of mourning, repentance, or devotion to prayer.

Thoughts

The early church changed the basic definition of what fasting was about. The church decided to adopt the Greek/Roman definition of fasting. This may have been done because of the view of fasting in the Mithras church that Paul was converting. It appears that during Yeshua's day there were people doing their voluntary fasting for the sake of making themselves look more righteous. It is possible that the use of sackcloth and ashes while fasting was developed by the religious leadership in order to elevate them to a high platform or higher position. The original intent of fasting was for Yom Kippur, the Day of Atonement. Over the centuries a view additional meaning were associated with fasting. By the time Yeshua arrived, the religious meaning of fasting had been expanded. So, Yeshua warned His followers not to show off their voluntary fasting. He did not outlaw the voluntary fasting. He wanted people to offer their devotion to God as something that existed only between the person and God.

Reflections

Fasting for spiritual purposes has always been somewhat blurry. Unfortunately, while fasting the thought of food keeps coming in my mind. The church says that fasting can bring you closer to God because you realize that you need food and that God does provide. The devote follower of Yeshua should know how to be humble before God through Yeshua's teaching. If fasting becomes a day of feeling hunger, then how can it help make devotions better. The hunger pangs will continue throughout the day. Therefore, giving oneself completed over to God at the time of fasting could become difficult when one is thinking about eating a meal. Distractions need to be avoided during prayer time. Fasting could easily create a distraction. Therefore, why does the church like to push fasting? It does appear to be a part of the Roman world and the Mithras religion. This could be another time that the early church accepted a cultural norm from society.

---

[i] *Sefer Ha-Zohar* (The Book of Radiance) is a mystical Torah commentary written in Aramaic. It comprises multiple volumes totaling over 1,000 pages.It is part of the corpus of the Jewish mystical tradition known as Kabbalah, though it is not the first work of that tradition, a distinction that belongs to the 12th-century *Sefer ha-Bahir* (The Book of Brilliance). The Zohar, however, is now one of the better-known works of kabbalistic literature, thanks to the early 20th-century scholarship of the German-born Israeli philosopher Gershom Scholem and to recent English translations. Though difficult to understand, due to the dense and obscure cosmological system the text inhabits, even in translation, the Zohar invites those willing to explore it into a fantastical universe filled with spiritual contemplation and insight. Source: https://www.myjewishlearning.com/article/the-zohar/

[ii] "The Jewish mystical doctrine known as "Kabbalah" (="Tradition") is distinguished by its theory of ten creative forces that intervene between the infinite, unknowable God ("Ein Sof") and our created world. Through these powers God created and rules the universe, and

it is by influencing them that humans cause God to send to Earth forces of compassion or severe judgment." Source: https://www.jewishvirtuallibrary.org/the-ten-sefirot-of-the-kabbalah

iii

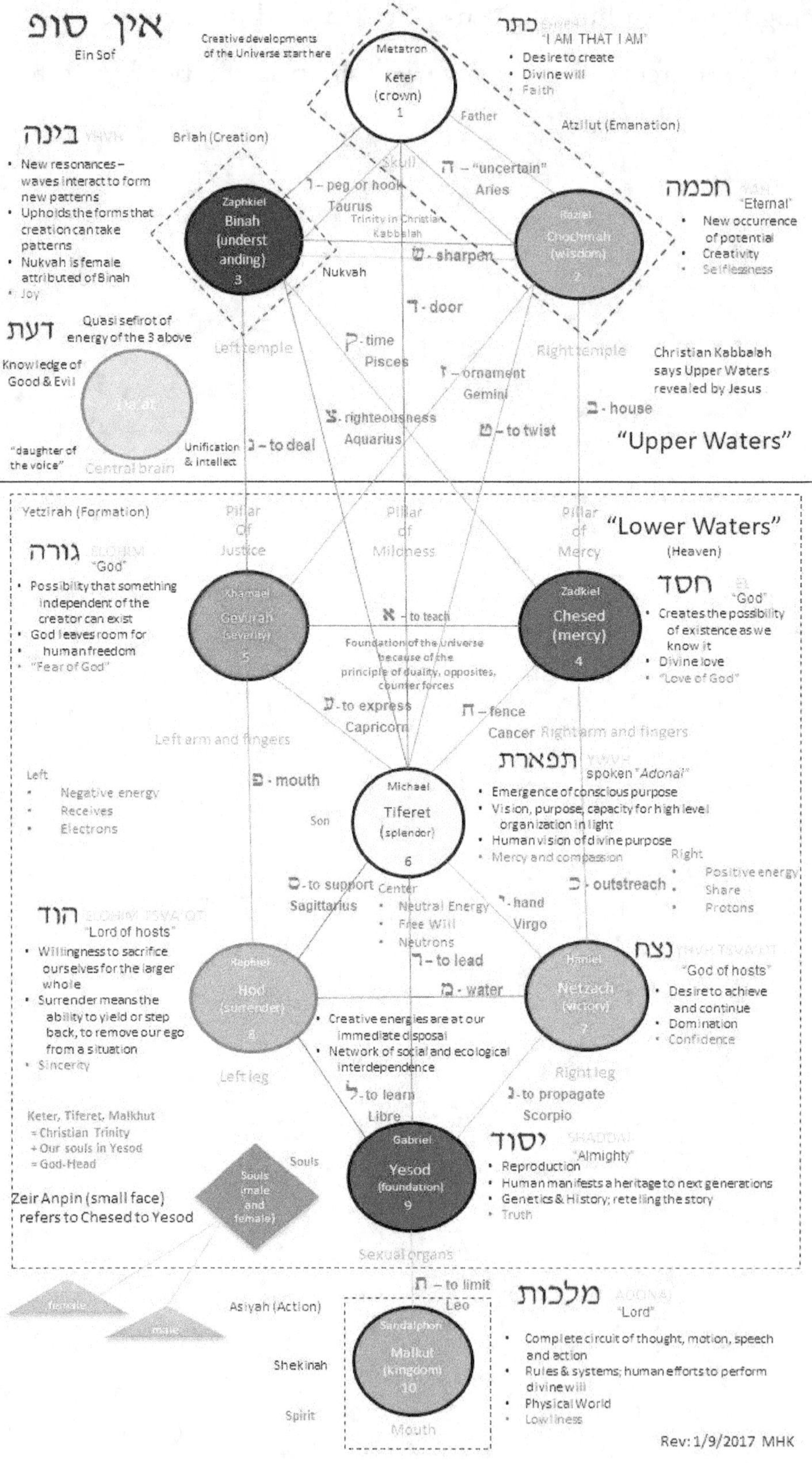
אין סוף
Ein Sof
Creative developments
of the Universe start here
כתר
"I AM THAT I AM"
• Desire to create
• Divine will
• Faith
Metatron
Keter
(crown)
1
Father
Atzilut (Emanation)
Briah (Creation)
Skull
ה – "uncertain"
Aries
בינה YHVH
• New resonances –
waves interact to form
new patterns
• Upholds the forms that
creation can take
patterns
• Nukvah is female
attributed of Binah
• Joy
ו – peg or hook
Taurus
Trinity in Christian
Kabbalah
Zaphkiel
Binah
(understanding)
3
Nukvah
ש – sharpen
Baziel
Chochmah
(wisdom)
2
חכמה
"Eternal"
• New occurrence
of potential
• Creativity
• Selflessness
דעת
Quasi sefirot of
energy of the 3 above
Knowledge of
Good & Evil
Daat
"daughter of
the voice"
Left temple
Central brain
Unification
& intellect
ד – door
ק – time
Pisces
ז – ornament
Gemini
Right temple
ב – house
Christian Kabbalah
says Upper Waters
revealed by Jesus
צ – righteousness
Aquarius
ג – to deal
ט – to twist
"Upper Waters"
Yetzirah (Formation)
Pillar
Of
Justice
Pillar
of
Mildness
Pillar
of
Mercy
"Lower Waters"
(Heaven)
גורה ELOHIM
"God"
• Possibility that something
independent of the
creator can exist
• God leaves room for
human freedom
• "Fear of God"
Khamael
Gevurah
(severity)
5
א – to teach
Foundation of the universe
because of the
principle of duality, opposites,
counter forces
Zadkiel
Chesed
(mercy)
4
חסד
EL
"God"
• Creates the possibility
of existence as we
know it
• Divine love
• "Love of God"
Left arm and fingers
ע – to express
Capricorn
ח – fence
Cancer Right arm and fingers
תפארת YHVH
spoken "Adonai"
• Emergence of conscious purpose
• Vision, purpose, capacity for high level
organization in light
• Human vision of divine purpose
• Mercy and compassion
Left
• Negative energy
• Receives
• Electrons
Michael
Tiferet
(splendor)
6
Son
פ – mouth
ס – to support Center
Sagittarius
• Neutral Energy
• Free Will
• Neutrons
ר – to lead
מ – water
י – hand
Virgo
כ – outstreach
Right
• Positive energy
• Share
• Protons
הוד ELOHIM TSVA OT
"Lord of hosts"
• Willingness to sacrifice
ourselves for the larger
whole
• Surrender means the
ability to yield or step
back, to remove our ego
from a situation
• Sincerity
Raphiel
Hod
(surrender)
8
Haniel
Netzach
(victory)
7
נצח YHVH TSVA OT
"God of hosts"
• Desire to achieve
and continue
• Domination
• Confidence
Left leg
Right leg
Keter, Tiferet, Malkhut
= Christian Trinity
+ Our souls in Yesod
= God-Head
Zeir Anpin (small face)
refers to Chesed to Yesod
Souls
Souls
(male
and
female)
ל – to learn
Libre
נ – to propagate
Scorpio
Gabriel
Yesod
(foundation)
9
יסוד SHADDAI
"Almighty"
• Reproduction
• Human manifests a heritage to next generations
• Genetics & History; retelling the story
• Truth
female
male
Sexual organs
ת – to limit
Leo
Asiyah (Action)
Shekinah
Spirit
Sandalphon
Malkut
(kingdom)
10
מלכות ADONAI
"Lord"
• Complete circuit of thought, motion, speech
and action
• Rules & systems; human efforts to perform
divine will
• Physical World
• Lowliness
Mouth
Rev: 1/9/2017 MHK

[iv] The majestic presence or manifestation of God which has descended to "dwell" among men. Source: http://www.jewishencyclopedia.com/articles/13537-shekinah

[v]

Chambers of Aba and Ima of Briyah

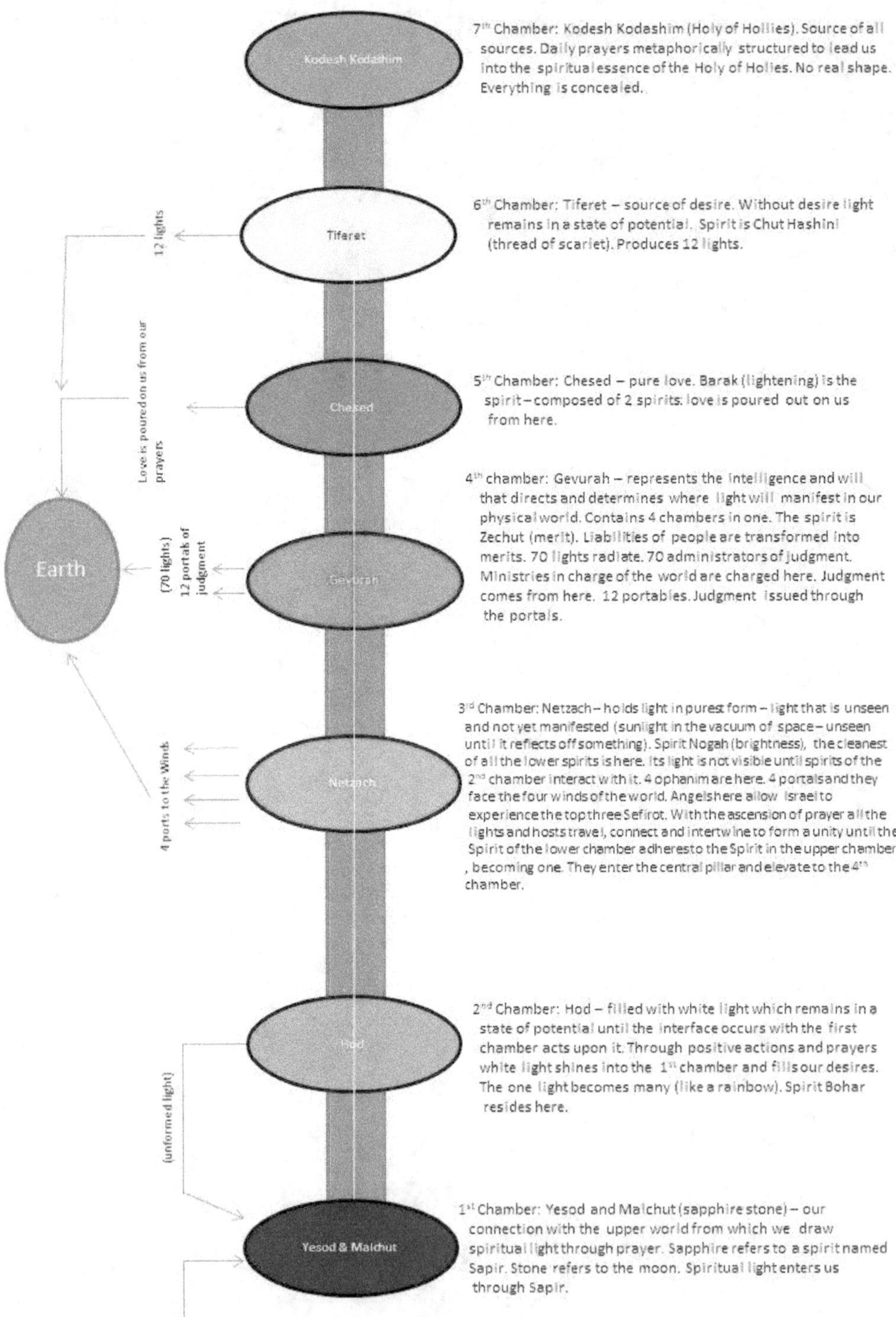

7th Chamber: Kodesh Kodashim (Holy of Hollies). Source of all sources. Daily prayers metaphorically structured to lead us into the spiritual essence of the Holy of Hollies. No real shape. Everything is concealed.

6th Chamber: Tiferet – source of desire. Without desire light remains in a state of potential. Spirit is Chut Hashini (thread of scarlet). Produces 12 lights.

5th Chamber: Chesed – pure love. Barak (lightening) is the spirit – composed of 2 spirits: love is poured out on us from here.

4th chamber: Gevurah – represents the intelligence and will that directs and determines where light will manifest in our physical world. Contains 4 chambers in one. The spirit is Zechut (merit). Liabilities of people are transformed into merits. 70 lights radiate. 70 administrators of judgment. Ministries in charge of the world are charged here. Judgment comes from here. 12 portables. Judgment issued through the portals.

3rd Chamber: Netzach – holds light in purest form – light that is unseen and not yet manifested (sunlight in the vacuum of space – unseen until it reflects off something). Spirit Nogah (brightness), the cleanest of all the lower spirits is here. Its light is not visible until spirits of the 2nd chamber interact with it. 4 ophanim are here. 4 portals and they face the four winds of the world. Angels here allow Israel to experience the top three Sefirot. With the ascension of prayer all the lights and hosts travel, connect and intertwine to form a unity until the Spirit of the lower chamber adheres to the Spirit in the upper chamber, becoming one. They enter the central pillar and elevate to the 4th chamber.

2nd Chamber: Hod – filled with white light which remains in a state of potential until the interface occurs with the first chamber acts upon it. Through positive actions and prayers white light shines into the 1st chamber and fills our desires. The one light becomes many (like a rainbow). Spirit Bohar resides here.

1st Chamber: Yesod and Malchut (sapphire stone) – our connection with the upper world from which we draw spiritual light through prayer. Sapphire refers to a spirit named Sapir. Stone refers to the moon. Spiritual light enters us through Sapir.

Our prayers enter the 1st chamber and can draw spiritual light from it.

Matthew 6:19-21

Language

New American Standard 1995	Koine Greek
[19] "Do not store up for yourselves treasures on earth, where moth and rust destroy, and where thieves break in and steal. [20] "But store up for yourselves treasures in heaven, where neither moth nor rust destroys, and where thieves do not break in or steal; [21] for where your treasure is, there your heart will be also.	[19] Μὴ θησαυρίζετε ὑμῖν θησαυροὺς ἐπὶ τῆς γῆς, ὅπου σὴς καὶ βρῶσις ἀφανίζει, καὶ ὅπου κλέπται διορύσσουσιν καὶ κλέπτουσιν· [20] θησαυρίζετε δὲ ὑμῖν θησαυροὺς ἐν οὐρανῷ, ὅπου οὔτε σὴς οὔτε βρῶσις ἀφανίζει, καὶ ὅπου κλέπται οὐ διορύσσουσιν οὐδὲ κλέπτουσιν. [21] Ὅπου γάρ ἐστιν ὁ θησαυρὸς ὑμῶν, ἐκεῖ ἔσται καὶ ἡ καρδία ὑμῶν.

Process of Discovery

Linguistics Section

Linguistic Structure

A [19] "Do not store up for yourselves treasures on earth,

  B' where moth and rust destroy, and where thieves break in and steal.

A' [20] "But store up for yourselves treasures in heaven,

  B' where neither moth nor rust destroys, and where thieves do not break in or steal;

[Proverb] [21] for where your treasure is, there your heart will be also.

Discussion

This is a simple statement that Yeshua made. The A-B-A'-B' chiasm is an introduction to the proverb in verse 21.

Questioning the Passage

1. What kind of treasures is Yeshua referring to?

    "Treasures in Heaven" refers to good deeds, and acts of kindness that are performed by an individual. These types of deeds are never forgotten and never perish. Earthly treasures are temporal, while Heavenly treasures are eternal.

    A connection between Matthew 6:1-16 and this passage is that the three pieties that Yeshua spoke do create treasures in Heaven.

2. What does the proverb of verse 21 mean?

    "The main and central organ of the body is a well-known metaphor for the center of a person's inner being (J. Behm, *TDNT* 3:605–14) and thus the center of a person's attention and commitment. With this compare the earlier uses of καρδία in the sermon (5:8, 28). Truly, the one who piles up treasures on earth will have his or her attention and commitment necessarily turned to earthly matters rather than to the will of the Father in heaven (cf. Luke 12:21)."[45]

    A person's actions and words are an expression of what they value. People who attend church and give the least amount they can to the work of Yeshua are telling Yeshua how much they love Him compared to Earthly things. The LORD calls for a tithing. Those who do not tithe are telling the LORD they love other things. This is a prelude

---

[45] Hagner, D. A. (1998). *Matthew 1–13* (Vol. 33A, p. 158). Dallas: Word, Incorporated.

to the upcoming discussion in Matthew's Gospel about serving money versus serving the LORD.

Phrase Study

1. βρῶσις ἀφανίζει (Matt. 6:19 BYZ)

   This phrase is usually translated as "rust destroys." The main translation for βρῶσις is "eating" or "food." Since the verse is speaking about moths and that people would hide their finest clothing in areas of the house where moths could live, the better translation is "where moths can eat to destroy." Thus, Yeshua is referring to the treasures on Earth that can lose their value over time. A modern example is gold and silver. Five or so years ago gold was selling at $1850 dollars (approximate) per troy ounce. Today it is selling for $1120 (approximate) per troy ounce.

Scripture cross references

Verse 19	Pro 23:4; Mat 19:21; Luk 12:21, Luk 12:33; Luk 18:22; 1Ti 6:9, 1Ti 6:10; Heb 13:5; Jam 5:2
Verse 20	Luk 12:33; 1Ti 6:19
Verse 21	Luk 12:34

Linguistic Echo

1. [4] Do not weary yourself to gain wealth, Cease from your consideration *of it*. (Prov. 23:4 NAU)

   Yeshua is echoing this Proverb verse. The people are warned by the writer of the Proverb that chasing after Earthly wealth does not insure anything beyond a life on Earth. Wealth can offer a better lifestyle on Earth but what will happen when the person reaches Heaven? It is better to execute acts of kindness that will give an eternal reward.

Culture Section

Discussion

During Yeshua's time there were no banks or safes to place valuables of silver and gold. In Yeshua's time people would bury their treasures (valuables) in the ground to keep them safe from bandits and robbers. They would also hide their costly garments and perishable goods in secret places constructed in the home (the inner room of the house and inside the walls). The treasures hidden in the walls may escape from robbers, but moths could easily reach the treasures. The ground in which homes were built upon were always damp and insects infested homes.

Near Easterners dream of discovering buried treasures. Since people buried their treasures it was common to discover hidden treasures. If such a discovery was made the treasure became the property of the person who found it no matter who owned it. Treasures would be buried at night, so the location could remain a secret. Unfortunately, if the person who buried the treasure died the treasure would be virtually lost to the family.

If a person happened to find a treasure in his neighbor's field, he hastened to buy the field to get possession of the treasure. If the government found out about the treasure a government official would arrive to confiscate it. Some people hid treasures while others searched for it.[46]

---

[46] Errico, Rocco A., and George M. Lamsa. Aramaic Light on the Gospel of Matthew: a Commentary on the Teachings of Jesus from the Aramaic and Unchanged Near Eastern Customs. Noohra Foundation, 2000.

Culture and Linguistics Section

Discussion

"The World to Come usually refers to one of three things: the way the world will be in the End of Days when the righteous are resurrected; a world of immortal souls that will follow the age of resurrection; or a heavenly world enjoyed by righteous souls immediately after death (i.e. prior to the End of Days). However, believing that the World to Come refers to one of these does not necessarily entail a negative belief in the others."[47]

"The Purpose of This World is to Get to the Next

Moses Hayyim Luzzatto's *The Path of the Upright*, compiled in the eighteenth century, is typical of the other-worldly approach. Luzzatto begins his guide to holy living with these words: "It is the foundation of saintliness and the perfect worship of God for a man to realize what constitutes his duty in his world and to which aim he is required to direct all his endeavors throughout his life. Now our Sages, of blessed memory, have taught us that man was created only to find delight in the Lord and to bask in the radiance of His Shekhinah for this is the true happiness and the greatest of all possible delights. The real place in which such delight can be attained is the World to Come, for this has been prepared to this very purpose. But the way to attain to this desired goal is this world. This world, the Sages remark, is like a vestibule before the World to Come. The means by which man reaches this goal are the precepts God, blessed be He, has commanded us and the place in which the precepts are to be carried out is only in this world. Man is put here in order to earn with the means at his command the place that has been prepared for him in the World to Come.""[48]

---

[47] Jacobs, Louis. "The World to Come." My Jewish Learning. Accessed August 29, 2018. https://www.myjewishlearning.com/article/the-world-to-come/.
[48] IBID.

The following chart is a comparison of what the Mithras doctrine about the World to Come was. Mithras did not use the term World to Come, however it had a strong eschatological definition. It appears that the Christian view of eschatology may have had its origin in Mithras.

Mithras	Christianity
"The background of Mithraic eschatology was provided by that theory of the relation of the soul to the universe. It was believed that the soul descended at birth {from) the eternal home of light through the gate of Cancer, passing down through the seven planetary spheres to earth. As the soul passed through each stage it accumulated more and more impurity. It was possible for the initiate, while in his trial period on earth, to gain purity through the practice of courage and truth." After death there was judgment of the soul. Mithra, the protector of the truth, presided over the judgment court. If the soul had lived an impure life, it was dragged down to the infernal depths, where it received a thousand tortures. If, on the contrary, its good qualities outweighed the bad, it rises through the gate of caprocorn, passing in reverse order through	Soul descends from Heaven. Augustine's doctrine of the soul is born in sin and needs immediate baptism. Treasures in Heaven. Judgment of the soul after death Evil people are condemned to Hell.

the planetary sphere. At each stage the impurities which the soul picked up in its downward flow gradually diminished. The end of this great rise was supreme happiness and eternal bliss. The doctrine of resurrection of the flesh was also a basic belief in the Mithraic circle."[49]	The Christian addition is that it is belief in Jesus that helps the person rise to heaven.

Thoughts

The idea of a World to Come, the end of time, is a concept that can be seen in the prophets, especially the minor prophets. By Yeshua's time this idea was a part of the religious culture. The Hebraic people would have been quite familiar with the idea of the World to Come. Why did Yeshua have to tell them about this? When reading the Sermon on the Mount there are places where the sermon jumps from topic to topic without a good connection between them. Matthew 6:1-18 is a discussion by Yeshua about the three pieties of His day. Then an abrupt change in direction to eschatology. Verse nineteen begins a section referring to what will happen when our time on Earth is complete. There is no transition or connection between the two topics. Also, the Hebraic people listening to Yeshua would have already known this. Perhaps, Yeshua says these things about the World to Come to emphasize them. In Hebraic beliefs the people were chosen by the LORD. Therefore, they do not need a savior because they are already saved. Once a year the people come before the LORD to confess their sins and ask for forgiveness (the purpose of Yom Kippur).

---

[49] Mithras. http://okra.stanford.edu/transcription/document_images/Vol01Scans/211_13Sept-23Nov1949_A%20Study%20of%20Mirthraism.pdf. August 29, 2018.

The early church arose out of the Mithras churches. Many pagans who were a part of the Mithras cult became the early churches. The Mithras belief in what happens after death clearly became a part of Christian doctrine. To authenticate the usage of the Mithras belief, the author of Matthew's Gospel had Yeshua affirm it. The early church, many of which were converted Mithras churches, maintained the pagan ways and simply used the writing of the Gospel to say that Yeshua said these things.

Reflections

This passage on treasures in Heaven could be viewed as the question from Yeshua, "What do you value the most?" This is the start of the passage that brings the question of how one can serve two masters, money or God, it would logical to view verses 19 through 21 as the start of the discussion. Which is more valuable to you, your treasures or God? Probably an overwhelming number of people who associate themselves with Christianity would say God. Then the question becomes, "how do you show this to God?" Since God knows what is in our heart and our actions reflect what is in our heart, it begs the question of how you show your love for God. The person who loves Yeshua but does not attend a worship celebration to Yeshua and does not follow the commandments of Yeshua, is clearly demonstrating that their earthly treasures are far more valuable than their acts of kindness that are done for God. When church goers put a dollar or two into the offering and call that 0.0001% of their income a tithe, are they showing their love to God? God asks that He may take back ten percent of what is His. "When surveyed, 17% of Americans state that they regularly tithe. For families making $75k+, 1% of them gave at least 10% in tithing."[50] It is clear there are very few people who value God more than their earthly

---

[50] https://www.google.com/search?source=hp&ei=gKaGW--IAoL6-QbYhIWgCA&q=average+tithing+to+church&btnK=Google+Search&oq=average+tithing+to+church&gs_l=psy-ab.3..0.207.4640..4828...0.0..1.495.6321.2-23j0j1......0....1..gws-wiz.....0..35i39j0i131j0i131i20i264j0i20i264j0i22i30.IN4J2337cF0

treasures. The question of money vs. God starts with treasures on Earth vs. treasures in Heaven.

Matthew 6:22-24

Language

New American Standard 1995	Koine Greek
[22] "The eye is the lamp of the body; so then if your eye is clear, your whole body will be full of light. [23] "But if your eye is bad, your whole body will be full of darkness. If then the light that is in you is darkness, how great is the darkness! [24] "No one can serve two masters; for either he will hate the one and love the other, or he will be devoted to one and despise the other. You cannot serve God and wealth.	[22] Ὁ λύχνος τοῦ σώματός ἐστιν ὁ ὀφθαλμός· ἐὰν οὖν ὁ ὀφθαλμός σου ἁπλοῦς ᾖ, ὅλον τὸ σῶμά σου φωτεινὸν ἔσται· [23] ἐὰν δὲ ὁ ὀφθαλμός σου πονηρὸς ᾖ, ὅλον τὸ σῶμά σου σκοτεινὸν ἔσται. Εἰ οὖν τὸ φῶς τὸ ἐν σοὶ σκότος ἐστίν, τὸ σκότος πόσον; [24] Οὐδεὶς δύναται δυσὶν κυρίοις δουλεύειν· ἢ γὰρ τὸν ἕνα μισήσει, καὶ τὸν ἕτερον ἀγαπήσει· ἢ ἑνὸς ἀνθέξεται, καὶ τοῦ ἑτέρου καταφρονήσει. Οὐ δύνασθε θεῷ δουλεύειν καὶ μαμωνᾷ.

Process of Discovery

Linguistics Section

Linguistic Structure

[Parable] [22] "The eye is the lamp of the body; so then if your eye is clear, your whole body will be full of light. [23] "But if your eye is bad, your whole body will be full of darkness. If then the light that is in you is darkness, how great is the darkness! [24] "No one can serve two masters; for either he will hate the one and love the other, or he will be devoted to one and despise the other. You cannot serve God and wealth.

Discussion

Verses 22 and 23 could be grouped together as a parable leaving verse 24 to stand alone. Another view is to see all three verses as being a part of the same parable. A possible reason for separating verse 24 from verse 22 and 23 is because it appears on the surface to have a change in topic.

Could verse 24 be a second concluding statement to the parable being presented? The simple answer is "yes." The complex answer is to show how they are connected. By understanding what the metaphors and culture expressed through the language gives a deeper understanding of the passage.

Questioning the Passage

1. What does the metaphor "lamp of the body" mean? (v. 22)

    The Word of God is often called a lamp because it illuminates the world and the ways of the LORD. The lamp of the body is the eye because there is a lot of sensory information that comes through the eye which illuminates the world to the person.

Culture Section

Discussion

A Pure Eye (clear eye) – a person with a "pure eye" is one who has no evil intention or ulterior motives to what they do or say. A "bad eye" is a person who is crafty and evil and has ulterior motives to what they say or do. Also, a cunning person who has a bad eye will call their evil ways "good." Yeshua is saying how much worse is an evil person's evil intentions when their good intentions are evil.[51]

---

[51] Errico, Rocco A., and George M. Lamsa. Aramaic Light on the Gospel of Matthew: A Commentary on the Teachings of Jesus from the Aramaic and Unchanged Near Eastern Customs. Santa Fe, NM: Noohra Foundation, 2000.

Two Masters – Near Eastern servants despise having to work for more than two masters. This can occur when the patriarch of the family dies and there are two or more brothers who take control of the family, the business, and the family's land. Generally, the Near Eastern family stays together even after the patriarch dies. Family tensions can rise as competition begins between the families that comprise the whole. Discrimination in the distribution of food and clothing can occur. In addition, jealousies and suspicions can arise causing domestic problems. If a servant demonstrates a courtesy or preference for one side of the family, the other side becomes angry. Shrewd servants will pretend to favor both families. Yeshua was saying that as servants one cannot serve God and worldly riches and pleasures at the same time. In His time Pharisees and priests showed the people how they loved the Torah, but they also loved gold, silver, and other means which gave them earthly wealth.[52]

Lumen internum (internal light) is a concept which was developed by Platonic-Stoic anthropology. It is a general belief that the divine lives in each person and directs us only to do good and to seek out good. There is a belief that the lumen internum can be turned to evil. It is not the eye itself which causes evil but rather the lumen internum turning into its opposite that causes a person to do evil.[53] There is a conflict with verse 23 because the interpretation of Yeshua's words is that it is the eye which is causing the evil. If the metaphors of the Aramaic language are used for the "clear eye" and "bad eye" then it is not the eye organ that causes the evil. The conflict is cleared, which results in the interpretation of the second half of verse 23 being the concept of lumen internum. Yeshua says that the light within a person turns to darkness. In other words, using the Greek concept, the lumen internum turns into its opposite. Since this is the way the church has interpreted this verse it divided verses 19-24 into three separate parts.

---

[52] IBID.
[53] Text and Interpretation Studies in the New Testament Presented to Matthew Black. Cambridge Univ Pr, 2009.

A Literal Parable Theological Interpretation

Verses 22 and 23 express the understanding that the eye is the lamp of the body. The eye sees everything that is going on around the body. It is the brain, the mind of the person viewing the world, which will determine what all the sensory input means and will put together a scenario of interpretation. The clear eye means that the person making the observations about his/her world sees the good and the bad. This person can see what actions other people do and whether those actions fit the Torah (the word of the LORD). The bad eye person will see the same world but will interpret evil intention as being good. Evil inclination infects such a person and forces the person to see evil as good as well as good intentions as being good. Once the mind is convinced that evil is good then everything the person does is good.

The idea of love and hate expressed in verse 24 are also biblical idioms for "choose" or "not to choose."[54] Every choice that a person makes demonstrates their desire for one outcome verses another outcome. Using the language of verse 24 the question could be raised, should one be loyal to God or loyal to earthly treasures. To see it is a bipolar way would be, loyal to God, or not loyal to God. That is the choice that Yeshua is talking about.

The "clear eye" person will choose to express their loyalty to God. The "bad eye" person will choose to express their loyalty to another other than God. The light is God while the darkness is Evil Inclination (or Satan). The love of God or earthly treasures is the same dichotomy. A person must choose. Light and darkness is a choice.

---

[54] The New Interpreter's Bible Commentary. Nashville: Abingdon Press, 2015.

Choosing God	Choosing Evil
Light	Darkness
Clear Eye	Bad Eye
Serve God	Desire earthly treasures

This parable feeds directly from verses 19 to 21, in which Yeshua talks about heavenly treasures and earthly treasures. If the last phrase of verse 24 is rewritten using God and treasures it would read:

You cannot desire both Heavenly treasures and Earthly treasures at the same time.

Serving Heavenly treasures can only occur if one is doing good things (mitzvot) that the LORD commands, then a person working to accumulate these treasures is serving God!

Therefore, Matthew 19-24 can be read as a single parable that has a lot of repetition on it.

A 19 "Do not store up for yourselves treasures on earth, where moth and rust destroy, and where thieves break in and steal.

B [20] "But store up for yourselves treasures in heaven, where neither moth nor rust destroys, and where thieves do not break in or steal; [21] for where your treasure is, there your heart will be also.

A' [22] "The eye is the lamp of the body; so then if your eye is clear, your whole body will be full of light.

B' [23] "But if your eye is bad, your whole body will be full of darkness. If then the light that is in you is darkness, how great is the darkness!

C [24] "No one can serve two masters; for either he will hate the one and love the other, or he will be devoted to one and despise the other.

C' You cannot serve God and wealth.

The grouping of verses 19-24 as one linguistic unit offers the chiastic structure shown above. The A block talks about the "light", that is the love of the LORD is discovered by a desire to serve to Him. The B block says that a darkness comes over the person who decides to not serve the LORD but rather an earthly item. This concept is repeated in block C where it is clearly stated that one cannot serve the LORD and serve earthly wealth at the same time. Divided loyalty does not work.

Yeshua make a clear argument that for a disciple of His one must be one hundred percent in favor of serving the LORD. There is no partially credit given to people who are disciples of the LORD when it suits. One is either serving the LORD or not. Those who serve the LORD will have treasures in heaven and the blessings of heaven upon them. Those who do not serve the LORD will have evil inclination always upon them.

An alternative chiasm is:

A' [1] "Beware of practicing your righteousness before men to be noticed by them; otherwise you have no reward with your Father who is in heaven. [2] "So when you give to the poor, do not sound a trumpet before you, as the hypocrites do in the synagogues and in the streets, so that they may be honored by men. Truly I say to you, they have their reward in full. [3] "But when you give to the poor, do not let your left hand know what your right hand is doing, [4] so that your giving will be in secret; and your Father who sees *what is done* in secret will reward you. [5] "When you pray, you are not to be like the hypocrites; for they love to stand and pray in the synagogues and on the street corners so that they may be seen by men. Truly I say to you, they have their reward in full. [6] "But you, when you pray, go into your inner room, close your door and pray to your Father who is in secret, and your Father who sees *what is done* in secret will reward you. [7] "And when you are praying, do not use meaningless repetition as the Gentiles do, for they suppose that they will be heard for their many words. [8] "So do not be like them; for your Father knows what you need before you ask Him. [9] "Pray, then, in this way: 'Our Father who is in heaven, Hallowed be Your name. [10] 'Your kingdom come. Your will be done, On earth as it is in heaven. [11] 'Give us this day our daily bread. [12] 'And forgive us our debts, as we also have forgiven our debtors. [13] 'And do not lead us into temptation, but deliver us from evil. *For Yours is the kingdom and the power and the glory forever. Amen* .' [14] "For if you forgive others for their transgressions, your heavenly Father will also forgive you. [15] "But if you do not forgive others, then your Father will not forgive your transgressions. [16] "Whenever you fast, do not put on a gloomy face as the hypocrites *do*, for they neglect their appearance so that they will be noticed by men when they are fasting. Truly I say to you, they have their reward in full. [17] "But you, when you fast, anoint your head and wash your face [18] so that your fasting will not be noticed by men, but by your Father who is in secret; and your Father who sees *what is done* in secret will reward you.

B [19] "Do not store up for yourselves treasures on earth, where moth and rust destroy, and where thieves break in and steal. [20] "But store up for yourselves treasures in heaven, where neither moth nor rust destroys, and where thieves do not break in or steal; [21] for where your treasure is, there your heart will be also.

A' [22] "The eye is the lamp of the body; so then if your eye is clear, your whole body will be full of light. [23] "But if your eye is bad, your whole body will be full of darkness. If then the light that is in you is darkness, how great is the darkness! [24] "No one can serve two masters; for either he will hate the one and love the other, or he will be devoted to one and despise the other. You cannot serve God and wealth.

Examining Matthew 6:1-24 as a section the chiasm is formed by the A block being actions that an individual can do to please the LORD and to create treasures in Heaven. The B block tells us that an individual must strive to create treasures in Heaven before concerning him/herself with treasures on earth. Eternity will be spent in Heaven, not on Earth.

A Midrash Interpretation of the Passage

The Hebraic midrash interpretation of verses 22-24 gives a different insight into the meaning of this passage. The Hebrew idiom a "clear eye" means "generosity," while a "bad eye" means "stinginess." The LORD wants His people to be generous with the blessings that He bestows. The more one gives away blessings the more one receives blessings.[55]

Proverbs 22:9 [WTT] טֽוֹב־עַיִן הוּא יְבֹרָךְ כִּי־נָתַן מִלַּחְמוֹ לַדָּֽל׃

[NAU] **Proverbs 22:9** He who is generous will be blessed, For he gives some of his food to the poor.

[TNK] **Proverbs 22:9** The generous man is blessed, For he gives of his bread to the poor.

---

[55] Goulder, Michael Douglas. Midrash and Lection in Matthew. London: SPCK, 1977.

Tov eyin, which are the first two words of this verse are translated as a "generous man." A "good eye" (the literal translation) is translated as an idiom. So, using the midrash and the idioms, verses 22 to 24 is saying that the generous person will be blessed while the stingy person will not be blessed. In this interpretation verse 24 is not saying that one has to a choice between God and money, but rather Yeshua is saying that one must decide whether to be generous and blessed or stingy and not blessed.

In churches today, this passage is linked with the yearly stewardship campaigns. The preacher usually berates the people to give a tithing to the church. Using the Greek understanding and the literal interpretation that is what the message becomes. The people tithed automatically in Yeshua's day. Therefore, there must be more to the passage. Using the Hebraic idioms and Midrash the passage is about generosity to the poor. One who gives to the poor will receive blessings from the LORD.

Thoughts

What started as a simple examination of the passage turned into a lot more than just the literal interpretation. The church has used the literal interpretation, especially verse 24, to guilt parishioners into giving more money to the church. At the literal surface that is what appears to be said by Yeshua. But the Hebrew people knew about the tithe and gave the tithe. If this is true, then why did Yeshua have to give a dichotomy of serving two masters. The depth of this passage contains more than the literal. Learning about the Hebraic idioms, that were transliterated into Koine Greek opens the meaning of the passage. Yeshua did not speak Greek, rather He spoke either Aramaic or Hebrew. Therefore, transliterating the Greek to Hebrew unlocks it. The clear (or good) eye and the bad eye idioms give the answer. The passage is about the blessings one receives from the LORD when being generous. The other way to deal with one's blessings from the LORD is to be stingy with them. An attitude of stinginess will block blessings from the LORD. Therefore, Yeshua tells us to be generous. Yeshua wants the best for us.

Reflections

This analysis was written in September of 2018. This passage has been used for years in the church to guilt people into giving more money to the operation of the church. The preacher says you cannot serve God and money and of course it is better to serve God. The response of the people is generally the same. That response is that nothing new happens. The generous people and the tithers continue to do what they were doing, and the stingy people give what they were giving. The tithers sit in the sermon wishing they did not have to hear the lecture about giving to the church because they do. The stringy people do not want to hear the lecture because they are intent on not giving a tithe or any amount close to it. When the church announces a consecration Sunday (a day to have people fill out commitment cards for the next year telling the church how much they will give) many people avoid church that day. Perhaps those who give so little to the church either do not value God compared to their earthly practices or they do not understand what the money is being used for. Unfortunately, the church does need money to operate. Also, the church cannot hold outreach projects to bring the Gospel of Yeshua to its community without funds. With the corruption seen in the hierarchy of the church perhaps there are people who do not want to support the organizational structure. One of the advantages of being a member of an independent church is that no money is going to support a hierarchy of bishops, cardinals and popes. When one sees the condition of several local Catholic churches in northern Mexico and then the money spent by the Vatican for vestments alone it makes one question how the money is being used. Do not think that this is a condemnation of only the catholic church. All the Christian denominations have this problem. Years ago, the bishop of the United Methodist church of the Baltimore-Washington area sat in his Herman Miller furnished office (about a $50,000 price tag) telling us to give more money to the church. Perhaps the tithing problem is a matter of trust. If the people in the pews had trust in the hierarchy and leadership of the church perhaps the fiscal problems would solve itself.

Matthew 6:25-34

Language

New American Standard 1995	Koine Greek
25 "For this reason I say to you, do not be worried about your life, *as to* what you will eat or what you will drink; nor for your body, *as to* what you will put on. Is not life more than food, and the body more than clothing? 26 "Look at the birds of the air, that they do not sow, nor reap nor gather into barns, and *yet* your heavenly Father feeds them. Are you not worth much more than they? 27 "And who of you by being worried can add a *single* hour to his life? 28 "And why are you worried about clothing? Observe how the lilies of the field grow; they do not toil nor do they spin, 29 yet I say to you that not even Solomon in all his glory clothed himself like one of these. 30 "But if God so clothes the grass of the field, which is *alive* today and tomorrow is thrown into the furnace, *will He* not much more *clothe* you? You of little faith! 31 "Do not worry then, saying, 'What will we eat?' or 'What will we drink?' or 'What will we wear for clothing?' 32 "For the Gentiles eagerly seek all these things; for your heavenly Father knows that you need all these things. 33 "But seek first His kingdom and His righteousness, and all these things will be added to you.	25 Διὰ τοῦτο λέγω ὑμῖν, μὴ μεριμνᾶτε τῇ ψυχῇ ὑμῶν τί φάγητε καὶ τί πίητε, μηδὲ τῷ σώματι ὑμῶν τί ἐνδύσεσθε οὐχὶ ἡ ψυχὴ πλείων ἐστι τῆς τροφῆς καὶ τὸ σῶμα τοῦ ἐνδύματος; 26 ἐμβλέψατε εἰς τὰ πετεινὰ τοῦ οὐρανοῦ, ὅτι οὐ σπείρουσιν οὐδὲ θερίζουσιν οὐδὲ συνάγουσιν εἰς ἀποθήκας, καὶ ὁ πατὴρ ὑμῶν ὁ οὐράνιος τρέφει αὐτά οὐχ ὑμεῖς μᾶλλον διαφέρετε αὐτῶν; 27 τίς δὲ ἐξ ὑμῶν μεριμνῶν δύναται προσθεῖναι ἐπὶ τὴν ἡλικίαν αὐτοῦ πῆχυν ἕνα; 28 καὶ περὶ ἐνδύματος τί μεριμνᾶτε; καταμάθετε τὰ κρίνα τοῦ ἀγροῦ πῶς αὐξάνει οὐ κοπιᾷ οὐδὲ νήθει 29 λέγω δὲ ὑμῖν ὅτι οὐδὲ Σολομὼν ἐν πάσῃ τῇ δόξῃ αὐτοῦ περιεβάλετο ὡς ἓν τούτων. 30 Εἰ δὲ τὸν χόρτον τοῦ ἀγροῦ, σήμερον ὄντα καὶ αὔριον εἰς κλίβανον βαλλόμενον, ὁ Θεὸς οὕτως ἀμφιέννυσιν, οὐ πολλῷ μᾶλλον ὑμᾶς, ὀλιγόπιστοι; 31 μὴ οὖν μεριμνήσητε λέγοντες, τί φάγωμεν ἢ τί πίωμεν ἢ τί περιβαλώμεθα; 32 πάντα γὰρ ταῦτα τὰ ἔθνη ἐπιζητεῖ οἶδε γὰρ ὁ πατὴρ ὑμῶν ὁ οὐράνιος ὅτι χρῄζετε τούτων ἁπάντων.

<table>
<tr><td>

[34] "So do not worry about tomorrow; for tomorrow will care for itself. Each day has enough trouble of its own.

</td><td>

[33] ζητεῖτε δὲ πρῶτον τὴν βασιλείαν τοῦ Θεοῦ καὶ τὴν δικαιοσύνην αὐτοῦ, καὶ ταῦτα πάντα προστεθήσεται ὑμῖν.
[34] Μὴ οὖν μεριμνήσητε εἰς τὴν αὔριον ἡ γὰρ αὔριον μεριμνήσει τὰ ἑαυτῆς ἀρκετὸν τῇ ἡμέρᾳ ἡ κακία αὐτῆς.

</td></tr>
</table>

Process of Discovery

Linguistics Section

Linguistic Structure

A 25 "For this reason I say to you, do not be worried about your life, *as to* what you will eat or what you will drink; nor for your body, *as to* what you will put on. Is not life more than food, and the body more than clothing?

> **B** [26] "Look at the birds of the air, that they do not sow, nor reap nor gather into barns, and *yet* your heavenly Father feeds them. Are you not worth much more than they?

>> **C** [27] "And who of you by being worried can add a *single* hour to his life? [28] "And why are you worried about clothing?

> **B'** Observe how the lilies of the field grow; they do not toil nor do they spin, [29] yet I say to you that not even Solomon in all his glory clothed himself like one of these. [30] "But if God so clothes the grass of the field, which is *alive* today and tomorrow is thrown into the furnace, *will He* not much more *clothe* you? You of little faith!

A' [31] "Do not worry then, saying, 'What will we eat?' or 'What will we drink?' or 'What will we wear for clothing?' [32] "For the Gentiles eagerly seek all these things; for your heavenly Father knows that you need all these things. [33] "But seek first His kingdom and His righteousness, and all these things will be added to you. [34] "So do not worry about tomorrow; for tomorrow will care for itself. Each day has enough trouble of its own.

Discussion

This is an A-B-C chiasm. The center of the chiasm is the question about adding time to one's life through worry.

Questioning the Passage

1. What does the smile to the birds of the air mean? (v. 26)

   This is a rhetorical question. The birds and other beasts on the Earth are important to God. He attends to the needs of them. Humans are more valuable to God then the birds. Therefore, Yeshua reminds us that our needs will be attended to.

2. What does the simile about the lilies mean? (v. 28)

   The words "toil or spin" is a reference to the need for humans to make their own clothing. The lilies in the valley are not in need of clothes. If the lilies need some type of covering, then God would supply it. Since humans require clothing, Yeshua is telling them not to worry for God provides. Clothing was an expensive commodity in Yeshua's day. If a person owned two sets of clothing, he/she was considered well off financially. Most people did not own two sets of clothing. They became concerned that when attending a wedding or a religious event they might not be dressed well. Yeshua could be making it clear that the appearance of the clothing of a person does not matter if the person is worshiping and trusting in God.

Alternate view

1. ^{NAU} **Matthew 6:27** "And who of you by being worried can add a *single* hour to his life? (Matt. 6:27 NAU)

πῆχυν translated into English means "cubit." A cubit was a unit of measure. Also, the word δύναται means "to be powerful." Using this translation, the question of verse twenty-seven could be posed as "And who of you are worried about having the power to add a cubit to your height in your lifetime." Once matured the body stops growing taller and there is nothing you can do about it. Therefore, why be concerned that you cannot do it. Perhaps an understanding that there are forces in the world we cannot see nor; can we do anything about it. For example, when a hurricane approaches the coast, humans cannot change the direction of the storm. One can prepare for it. One can leave the area. But one cannot change what will happen.

Scripture cross references

Verse 29   1Ki 10:4-7; 2Ch 9:4-6, 2Ch 9:20-22

Verse 30   Jam 1:10, Jam 1:11; 1Pe 1:24

Linguistic Echoes

1. [25] "For this reason I say to you, do not be worried about your life, *as to* what you will eat or what you will drink; nor for your body, *as to* what you will put on. Is not life more than food, and the body more than clothing? (Matt. 6:25 NAU)

The echo is a reminder to the disciples that God did take care of Israel when they wandered in the wilderness of Sinai. Since God did take care of Israel, Yeshua is reminding them that He will take care of them.

[14] When the layer of dew evaporated, behold, on the surface of the wilderness there was a fine flake-like thing, fine as the frost on the ground. [15] When the sons of Israel saw *it*, they said to one another, "What is it?" For they did not

know what it was. And Moses said to them, "It is the bread which the LORD has given you to eat. (Exod. 16:14-15 NAU)

Culture Section

Questioning the passage

1. What does the reference to the grass which is thrown into a furnace mean in verse thirty?

The furnace is the translation used by the NAU committee. The Greek word κλίβανος can also be translated as "oven." Using this translation Yeshua was referring to the oven which was in the center of the house. They were approximately three feet in diameter. The oven was about five feet deep and lined with baked clay. Underground passages to the oven were built to allow air flow into the oven. When the oven was lit it required fuel. The fuel used was grass and manure that the women gathered from the fields. Once the oven was lit dry grass was added until the inside of the oven was well heated, and the clay turned white. Pots containing food were lowered into the oven. Dough was rolled until it was as thin as cardboard and clapped onto the smooth clay inside the oven. When the oven was not in use a large wooden cover was placed over it so that children could not fall into it. Yeshua's reference to the grass is the type of grass that women gathered for the oven. Yeshua emphasizes is that even grass that is one of the least important plants of God's creation has known God's care. If God cared for the grass that heated the homes, how much more does God care about people who were made in His image?[56]

2. What does verse 31 & 32 mean?

---

[56] Errico, Rocco A., and George M. Lamsa. Aramaic Light on the Gospel of Matthew: A Commentary on the Teachings of Jesus from the Aramaic and Unchanged Near Eastern Customs. Santa Fe, NM: Noohra Foundation, 2000.

The Peshitta (the Aramaic Bible) says "worldly people" rather than "Gentiles." This is because the reference that Yeshua is making applies to Jews as much as it does to Gentiles. Worldly people are looking for what their next meal will be and what clothing they will be wearing. The phrase "worldly" people refer to those who have no regard for religion and holiness and who value the pleasures of this life only. These people are not concerned about religion nor spirituality. A worldly person is anyone who puts materialism before spiritual matters. These people believe that life consists only of treasures, luxuries, and power. They have no interest in justice and mercy. They are not concerned about the world to come. Yeshua encouraged His disciples to seek the spiritual things of life. Also, Yeshua's disciples cannot denounce riches and accumulate them at the same time. Yeshua's disciples seek the kingdom of God first and foremost.[57]

Thoughts

This passage is a conclusion to the entire chapter. The discussion has focused around accumulating treasures in Heaven opposed to treasures on Earth. Yeshua repeats His belief in the accumulation of treasures in Heaven by comparing people who are concerned about earthly treasures and people who are concerned about spiritual treasures (heavenly treasures). What good is the accumulation of earthly treasures if one's spirit is lost because of neglect? For the person who trusts in God will not have to worry about their needs on Earth and will have heavenly treasures waiting. Is it wrong to have earthly treasures? Yeshua did not say that one cannot have heavenly treasures. Yeshua says that when earthly treasures are more important then there is a problem. Who comes first, God or the individual? An expression of which treasure is more important can be seen in the giving of tithes and generosity. The person who gives a meager amount of money to the operation

---

[57] IBID.

of the church and calls it a tithe is demonstrating a falsehood to God. Do not think that a 1% giving of income is a tithe. The Bible says tithing is 10%. To fulfill the promise let God take 10%. Allowing less is showing God that earthly treasures are more important.

Reflections

It is difficult to listen to a lecture from a person who is not following their words. For example, the person on their soap box preaching global warming who drives a gas guzzling car and does not have solar panels on their house. This is one example of so many. The person who hurts the church the most is the one preaching that they are true disciples of Jesus Christ but only attend church on Christmas and Easter and give a whopping $10 a year for the maintenance of the church. Really! The idea behind this passage is to trust God and show God where your treasures lie. "God knows our hearts" is from the Hebrew Scriptures and is an idiom meaning that God knows how we feel by our actions. How many church treasures and finance secretaries complain about the giving income of the church and are a part of the problem? Unfortunately, there are many churches that have financial officers who are some of the worst givers. At one church the Chairperson of the Trustees and by the incorporation papers of the church was the President of the church gave zero dollars. Yes, you read that correctly. He gave zero dollars. Then during the year, he would complain about the Trustees' budget. This person was very well off and had a career that generated a healthy income. Those who live in glass houses should not throw stones. But do not worry because God knows this person's heart and he might have a lot of earthly treasures but possibly few to no heavenly treasures.

Matthew 7:1-5

Language

New American Standard 1995	Koine Greek
[1] "Do not judge so that you will not be judged. [2] "For in the way you judge, you will be judged; and by your standard of measure, it will be measured to you. [3] "Why do you look at the speck that is in your brother's eye, but do not notice the log that is in your own eye? [4] "Or how can you say to your brother, 'Let me take the speck out of your eye,' and behold, the log is in your own eye? [5] "You hypocrite, first take the log out of your own eye, and then you will see clearly to take the speck out of your brother's eye.	[1] Μὴ κρίνετε, ἵνα μὴ κριθῆτε· [2] ἐν ᾧ γὰρ κρίματι κρίνετε, κριθήσεσθε· καὶ ἐν ᾧ μέτρῳ μετρεῖτε, μετρηθήσεται ὑμῖν. [3] Τί δὲ βλέπεις τὸ κάρφος τὸ ἐν τῷ ὀφθαλμῷ τοῦ ἀδελφοῦ σου, τὴν δὲ ἐν τῷ σῷ ὀφθαλμῷ δοκὸν οὐ κατανοεῖς; [4] Ἢ πῶς ἐρεῖς τῷ ἀδελφῷ σου, Ἄφες ἐκβάλω τὸ κάρφος ἀπὸ τοῦ ὀφθαλμοῦ σου· καὶ ἰδού, ἡ δοκὸς ἐν τῷ ὀφθαλμῷ σου; [5] Ὑποκριτά, ἔκβαλε πρῶτον τὴν δοκὸν ἐκ τοῦ ὀφθαλμοῦ σου, καὶ τότε διαβλέψεις ἐκβαλεῖν τὸ κάρφος ἐκ τοῦ ὀφθαλμοῦ τοῦ ἀδελφοῦ σου. [6] Μὴ δῶτε τὸ ἅγιον τοῖς κυσίν· μηδὲ βάλητε τοὺς μαργαρίτας ὑμῶν ἔμπροσθεν τῶν χοίρων, μήποτε καταπατήσωσιν αὐτοὺς ἐν τοῖς ποσὶν αὐτῶν, καὶ στραφέντες ῥήξωσιν ὑμᾶς.

Process of Discovery

Linguistics Section

Linguistic Structure

[Statement] [1] "Do not judge so that you will not be judged.

[Repetition] [2] "For in the way you judge, you will be judged; and by your standard of measure, it will be measured to you.

[Repetition] [3] "Why do you look at the speck that is in your brother's eye, but do not notice the log that is in your own eye?

[Repetition] ⁴ "Or how can you say to your brother, 'Let me take the speck out of your eye,' and behold, the log is in your own eye?

[Repetition] ⁵ "You hypocrite, first take the log out of your own eye, and then you will see clearly to take the speck out of your brother's eye.

Discussion

Verse one is a simple statement. Yeshua decided to repeat the statement four times. It is interesting that this commandment had to be repeated so intensely.

Questioning the Passage[58]

1. What does it mean to judge another person? (v. 2)

   "Not judge" is the exact translation of the Koine Greek. It means not to judge peoples' habits, weaknesses, and actions. Yeshua knew that everyone has some sort of character defect and shortcomings. No one is perfect. Yeshua is censuring gossip, criticism and slander of others that usually result in quarrels.[59]

2. What is the reference to "your standard of measure" mean? (v. 2)

   Many of the merchants in Yeshua's day did not have precise measuring tools. Each merchant used his own standard of measurement. Merchants would use their arms to measure dry goods and large and small stones for weights. The measurement of a "cubit" is a good example. The cubit was a measurement from the elbow to the end of the longest finger. Thus, a cubit would vary between merchants.[60]

---

[58] (The questions and answers offered are for discussion purposes. You may have different questions and answers. Remember all questions are valid and all answers must be defendable from Scripture. This applies to this section and to the Culture Section.)

[59] Errico, Rocco A., and George M. Lamsa. Aramaic Light on the Gospel of Matthew: A Commentary on the Teachings of Jesus from the Aramaic and Unchanged Near Eastern Customs. Santa Fe, NM: Noohra Foundation, 2000.
[60] IBID.

3. What does the reference to the log mean? (v. 3 – 5)

   Yeshua is using exaggeration, which was done quite frequently in His day. Instead of finding fault with other people, one should look in the mirror and correct one's own faults.

Culture Section

Discussion

In the marketplace one could have seen how a merchant did their measurements. A saying of the day was "good measure, pressed down, shaken together, running over." The people believed that a friendship mingled with business. When liquids, such as milk and oil, was poured into a buyer's container the liquid had to run over at least a little bit because it was understood "for what measures you measure, it will be measured to you." When grain was purchased the merchant would pour grain into a measuring square, made of wood. He would whirl the wheat in the box several times. Then using his hands, palms down, he would press it, and shake it up, until the grain overflowed the rim of the container.

When measuring goods, like cloths, the merchant used his arms to measure. Since people had different length arms this caused problems. Two men working together as merchants of cloth would make a lot of money if one had long arms, he would buy cloth, and the selling merchant had short arms. Sometimes in a transaction the buyer would insist that his/her arm length be used especially if they had long arms.

Yeshua knew of the practices of merchants using short arms and not shaking the measuring boxes. He knew that this idea of cheating was seen in human relationships. Yeshua was also referring to being generous is a component of a true spiritual life in verses one and two.

Thoughts

This section can be equated to Yeshua's golden rule. Using the culture of measurements and standards Yeshua is saying that if you do not want to be cheated then you must not cheat others. So, treat others in the same manner that you want to be treated. This includes judging people. If you do not want to be judged for your faults, then you must not find fault in others. Everyone has faults. No one is perfect, except Yeshua. The only way for a community to survive is to ensure that the relations between people stay intact. Therefore, not judging other peoples' habits, whether good or bad, is important to this understanding. Community was important to Yeshua and can be seen in this passage and in many other passages. Look into the mirror and notice your faults before you condemn others about theirs.

Reflections

When this passage is read the people usually think about the judgment of sin. It is God who judges if a person is sinful. Yeshua was not looking at the sins of people in this passage. Rather, He was talking about judging peoples' habits and lifestyle. It is not fair to judge someone else's life decisions. We have been given free will by the LORD and it is each of our decisions to what we do with this freedom. It is not proper, according to Yeshua, for anyone to look down upon a person's decision as to what they will do with that freedom. Many times, a person does not have all the information about a situation and can make a bad decision. To avoid this possibility, it is better not to judge anyone else. Clearly Yeshua is talking about keeping a community together. Gossip is a quick community killer especially when it is fake news. There is too much fake news coming out of most of America's media outlets. Too many rumors and gossip about people. Why do people listen to the fake news and take it as the gospel? Yeshua is saying that we must stop gossip. We must not listen to gossip. We certainly must not spread gossip.

Matthew 7:6

Language

New American Standard 1995	Koine Greek
[6] "Do not give what is holy to dogs, and do not throw your pearls before swine, or they will trample them under their feet, and turn and tear you to pieces.	Μὴ δῶτε τὸ ἅγιον τοῖς κυσίν· μηδὲ βάλητε τοὺς μαργαρίτας ὑμῶν ἔμπροσθεν τῶν χοίρων, μήποτε καταπατήσωσιν αὐτοὺς ἐν τοῖς ποσὶν αὐτῶν, καὶ στραφέντες ῥήξωσιν ὑμᾶς.

Process of Discovery

Linguistics Section

Linguistic Structure

[Parable] [6] Do not give what is holy to dogs, and do not throw your pearls before swine, or they will trample them under their feet, and turn and tear you to pieces.

Questioning the Passage

1. What is holy?

   Anything defined as clean in the Torah, that is dedicated and consecrated to the LORD was considered holy. Items and animals that were considered unclean could not be made holy. Yeshua was referring to the Torah and His Gospel as being Holy.

Culture Section

Discussion

Dogs were considered unclean animals, but swine were an abomination to Jews. Even today Jews do not pork and despise dogs. According to Semitic custom the less a wise man speaks the more people will honor him. The pearls of wisdom that he says will spread everywhere. Wise men usually spoke with other wise men. Wise men did not like discussing deep subjects with men who were not his equal. If they were in the company of uncultured people they would rather sit quietly and listen to the foolish talk, rather than say something that the people would not understand.

During debates on theological and philosophical questions bitter words were usually exchanged. Each person believed that he was correct and refused to admit he was wrong. When a learned man failed to defend his position, he could verbally attack the wise man. This was done so that he could avenge his honor. Men of wisdom tolerated each other and when their position was not correct they were willing to accept the verdict of others.

Yeshua was warning his disciples not to discuss theology and philosophy with people who would not understand. Misunderstandings could create disputes which could cause a fight to break out. Unlearned persons were like swine who would tread on the pearls of wisdom that are placed under their feet. Yeshua preached His gospel using simple illustrations from daily life and parables, so that people could understand. He told his disciples to do the same thing.[61]

Church Usage

According to the Didache 9:5, people who not baptized were not permitted to be a part of the communion feast or sacrament.

> 9:5. But let none eat or drink of your Eucharist except those who have been baptized in the Lord's Name. For concerning this also did the Lord say, "Give not that which is holy to the dogs.

Throughout the centuries this idea has been used to make the church seem like an elitist organization.

---

[61] Errico, Rocco A., and George M. Lamsa. *Aramaic Light on the Gospel of Matthew: A Commentary on the Teachings of Jesus from the Aramaic and Unchanged Near Eastern Customs.* Santa Fe, NM: Noohra Foundation, 2000.

Thoughts

What did Yeshua mean by this statement? He was warning his disciples not to engage in a discussion about the Gospels with anyone who was going to get agitated by His words to the point of violence. Yeshua knows that there are people in the world who will never accept His Gospel and they will not want to hear His words. Instead of getting into an argument and possible fight with such people it is better to walk away. Dogs will tear their food into pieces and this metaphor is about a person will start a physical fight to say that the Gospel is false. Swine will step on anything and because of their weigh will destroy it. The pearls can be a metaphor for the words of Yeshua and having these words destroyed by non-believers is not something that pleases Yeshua. One should introduce a person to the Gospel. If their reaction is completely negative to the point of hostilities, then Yeshua says walk away.

Reflections

There are people in the church today who this verse applies to. They do not want to hear the words of Yeshua, rather they want to hear that they are saved no matter what they say or do. Biblical preaching is hard to find in churches because the people who are the loudest in their complaints are the people who do not want to hear Yeshua's words. They want to hear nice stories about how much God loves them. It is sad that there are many preachers of the Gospel who tell nice stories and conclude with Yeshua loves them. They never preach the Gospel because they do not want to deal with the consequences of telling Yeshua's true word. There is no value to preaching the Gospel to people who do not want to hear it. Saddest is that occurs in churches. Yeshua's words are tough and many times act like a double-edged sword. However, Yeshua wants them to be heard. True disciples of Yeshua want to hear the words, all of them, because following everything Yeshua said makes one a better person and better prepared for Heaven.

Matthew 7:7-12

Language

New American Standard 1995	Koine Greek
[7] "Ask, and it will be given to you; seek, and you will find; knock, and it will be opened to you. [8] "For everyone who asks receives, and he who seeks finds, and to him who knocks it will be opened. [9] "Or what man is there among you who, when his son asks for a loaf, will give him a stone? [10] "Or if he asks for a fish, he will not give him a snake, will he? [11] "If you then, being evil, know how to give good gifts to your children, how much more will your Father who is in heaven give what is good to those who ask Him! [12] "In everything, therefore, treat people the same way you want them to treat you, for this is the Law and the Prophets.	[7] Αἰτεῖτε, καὶ δοθήσεται ὑμῖν· ζητεῖτε, καὶ εὑρήσετε· κρούετε, καὶ ἀνοιγήσεται ὑμῖν. [8] Πᾶς γὰρ ὁ αἰτῶν λαμβάνει, καὶ ὁ ζητῶν εὑρίσκει, καὶ τῷ κρούοντι ἀνοιγήσεται. [9] Ἢ τίς ἐστιν ἐξ ὑμῶν ἄνθρωπος, ὃν ἐὰν αἰτήσῃ ὁ υἱὸς αὐτοῦ ἄρτον, μὴ λίθον ἐπιδώσει αὐτῷ; [10] Καὶ ἐὰν ἰχθὺν αἰτήσῃ, μὴ ὄφιν ἐπιδώσει αὐτῷ; [11] Εἰ οὖν ὑμεῖς, πονηροὶ ὄντες, οἴδατε δόματα ἀγαθὰ διδόναι τοῖς τέκνοις ὑμῶν, πόσῳ μᾶλλον ὁ πατὴρ ὑμῶν ὁ ἐν τοῖς οὐρανοῖς δώσει ἀγαθὰ τοῖς αἰτοῦσιν αὐτόν; [12] Πάντα οὖν ὅσα ἂν θέλητε ἵνα ποιῶσιν ὑμῖν οἱ ἄνθρωποι, οὕτως καὶ ὑμεῖς ποιεῖτε αὐτοῖς· οὗτος γάρ ἐστιν ὁ νόμος καὶ οἱ προφῆται.

Process of Discovery

Linguistics Section

Linguistic Structure

[Ask and receive] [7] "Ask, and it will be given to you; seek, and you will find; knock, and it will be opened to you. [8] "For everyone who asks receives, and he who seeks finds, and to him who knocks it will be opened.

[Ask and receive] [9] "Or what man is there among you who, when his son asks for a loaf, will give him a stone? [10] "Or if he asks for a fish, he will not give him a snake, will he? [11] "If you then, being evil, know how to give good gifts to your children, how much more will your Father who is in heaven give what is good to those who ask Him!

[Golden Rule] [12] "In everything, therefore, treat people the same way you want them to treat you, for this is the Law and the Prophets.

Discussion

The passage is composed of two actions and the Golden Rule with internal repetition.

Questioning the Passage

1. What does "ask, seek and knock" mean? (v. 7)

   Yeshua decided at this point in the Sermon on the Mount to talk about prayer. His disciples were to be instructed in prayer because prayer is the communication device used to be in contact with the LORD.

   There were three components to Hebraic prayer in Yeshua's day. The first part was to ask the LORD. The second part was to seek the LORD's will and direction. The third part was to knock on the doors of mercy. These are three Hebraic expressions of prayer. They are not necessarily done together or tied together in any way. Prayer is a quest and an expectation, to bring human needs to the LORD but is not to inform the LORD of one's needs. Prayer is showing one's relationship to the LORD and to demonstrate ones' dependency on the LORD.[62]

2. What is the Golden Rule as offered in verse twelve?

This is a core issue and teaching of the Law and the Prophets. If all humankind followed this verse there would be no need for laws because evil would cease. The verse says that one's behavior can boomerang to the person who initiates the behavior. For example, the oppressor one day can become the oppressed; injustices committed could be done to the person committing the injustice; those who live by the sword will die by the sword.[63]

The Golden Rule appeared in Hebraic writings as early as the book of Tobit (written in the third century BCE).

[15] And what you hate, do not do to anyone. (Tob. 4:15 NRS)

The Greek philosopher Isocrates (born 436 BCE) was one of the first philosophers to offer a Golden Rule. Isocrates Golden Rule was created to tell the people that they needed to keep a good relationship with their ruler or else their ruler would inflict pain and suffering on them.[64]

---

[62] The New Interpreter's Bible. Nashville: Abingdon Press, 2006.
[63] Stern, David H. *Jewish New Testament Commentary*. Clarksville, MD: Jewish New Testament Publications, 1999.
[64] Wattles, Jeffrey. The Golden Rule. New York: Oxford University Press, 1996.

Aristotle's (born 384 BCE) Golden rule was: "Perfect friendship is the friendship of good men and of men who are similar according to their virtue. For they wish things that are good similarly to each other as good men they are essentially good."[65]

In the Far East the philosopher Confucius wrote done his Golden Rule.[66] Yeshua's Golden rule is a paraphrase of Leviticus 19:18.

> [18] 'You shall not take vengeance, nor bear any grudge against the sons of your people, but you shall love your neighbor as yourself; I am the LORD. (Lev. 19:18 NAU)

The difference between Yeshua's Golden Rule and other Golden Rules is that Yeshua stated it in a positive way:

> [12] "In everything, therefore, treat people the same way you want them to treat you, for this is the Law and the Prophets. (Matt. 7:12 NAU)

Linguistic Echoes

1. Verse 12, the Golden Rule, is a positive restatement of Leviticus 19:18.

Culture Section

Questioning the passage

1. What is the metaphorical significance of verse nine?

   In the Middle East people who lived in tents would keep their bread in a pile of stones around their tents. It was possible that a person would have been apt to pick up a

---

[65] Chilton, Bruce, and Jacob Neusner. The Golden Rule: The Ethics of Reciprocity in World Religions. London: Continuum, 2008.

[66] Freedman, Russell, and Frédéric Clément. Confucius: The Golden Rule. New York: Scholastic, 2003.

stone instead of bread by mistake. The bread and stones closely resembled each other in shape and size. People in Yeshua's day ate when they were hungry during the day or night.[67]

2. What is the metaphorical significance of verse ten?

Houses were constructed in Yeshua's day loosely and could have large holes and cracks in the walls. Birds and snakes could build their nests in the ceiling because the roofs were built with brush and straw. It was common to see snakes crawling along the ceiling and dropping to the floor. When fish was cooked it was placed in a basket. The aroma drew snakes and insects to the basket. It was common when taking a fish out of the basket to grab a snake that crawled into the basket. Yeshua was using his culture to explain that a loving father would check what he gave his children. Since most houses did not have lamps, it was important to double check what was pulled out of the basket.[68]

3. Was Yeshua calling all people evil? (v. 11)

Yeshua was not calling all people evil. "Being evil" meant that people make mistakes because of their imperfections. No one is perfect, and all people make mistakes. The imperfect parent knows how to give good gifts to their children. If the imperfect parent is careful to do the right thing, why would anyone doubt that God the Father, who is perfect, would only give perfect gifts.[69]

Culture and Linguistics Section

---

[67] Errico, Rocco A., and George M. Lamsa. Aramaic Light on the Gospel of Matthew: A Commentary on the Teachings of Jesus from the Aramaic and Unchanged Near Eastern Customs. Santa Fe, NM: Noohra Foundation, 2000.
[68] IBID.
[69] IBID.

Discussion

Verses nine and ten's meaning and understanding in Yeshua's day is cleared up when the culture of the day is applied. The stones and bread are connected because of the way people stored their bread. The snake and fish are connected because snakes could get into the fish pots in the homes. So, when bread was removed from the pile or when fish was removed from the pot, the person removing the item would have to be careful of what they picked up.

Midrash

"Rabbi Hillel, the renowned teacher living in Palestine in the first century BCE, is credited as the original source of the Golden Rule. "What is hateful to you, do not do to your fellow: this is the whole Torah; the rest is the explanation; go and learn" Babylonian Talmud, Sabbath 31:1. According to the Midrash, a non-Jewish man said to Hillel, "He would convert if Hillel could explain Judaism while he stands on one foot." The man probably asked Hillel this question not expecting a meaningful answer, but Hillel responded with this insightful response, according to the Talmud.

Treating everyone with kindness in a loving way may not always be easy. One needs to acknowledge everyone's points of view and have compassion even when exhausted, angry or feeling low. That compassion may lift your own spirits and influence others to mirror your actions."[70]

Zohar

---

[70] Author. "Tag: Golden Rule." Hebrew Seminary. Accessed September 26, 2018.
https://blog.hebrewseminary.org/tag/golden-rule/.

"Loving our neighbor is how we discover our own divinity and in turn our connection to the Light. **To love thy neighbor as thyself is the key that unlocks the greatest of treasures: The bounty of fulfillment which the Creator seeks only to impart upon us.**"[71]

Thoughts

The idea of a Golden Rule has been around for quite a long time. From the beginning of human civilization in the Mesopotamian Valley in the Middle East people have been fighting against each other and killing each other because they either could not get along with each other or they could not share their resources. All people whose ancestors originate in the Middle East are connected to each other. Some of the DNA links are probably very diluted, but nonetheless we are connected. Better is to go back further to discover that humans originated in Africa as a single tribe and then multiplied and migrated. It is sad that as cities were developed, then nations, then Empires, that one group of people desired dominance over another. Why do certain people have this idea to dominate others? In the 20th century two devasting world wars were fought because one group thought that it was better than the rest of the world. Since we are made in the LORD's image we are all equal. The diversity that we have is a gift from the LORD. What would the world be if we all looked alike, sounded alike and behaved alike? That sounds too boring to contemplate. One thing is for sure it is human diversity which allows for scientific discovery. Our differences allow some of us to have different talents and abilities. As Saint Paul said the church is composed of people of different abilities and talents. Tying us together is our connection to Yeshua.

---

71 "Acharei Mot-Kedoshim: The Secret of the Golden Rule." The Kabbalah Centre. Accessed September 26, 2018. https://kabbalah.com/en/concepts/acharei-mot-kedoshim-the-secret-of-the-golden-rule.

Reflections

It is frightening to see the reaction of the members of two churches when the leadership begins the discussion of merging together. The Golden Rule becomes a hunk of rusted iron that is discarded even before the presentation for the positives for a merge ends. Then the battle lines get drawn. There are always people who like the idea of coming together as a larger stronger church. Then the small number of objectors develop their smear strategy to stop the leadership from doing it. Even if the church votes for the merger the losers create even more static, smears and noise, that the majority eventually caves in and gives the loser their way. The resistance to the merger forgets the words of Yeshua about loving one another and working together for the good of the Gospel. This is a plain example of selfishness that occurs in the churches. Even two churches of the same denomination, whose leadership proposes a merger, will find that the actual process will get derailed by the objectors. Why is it that the words of Yeshua are so many times lost in Yeshua's churches? It is not just the topic of merger that causes it. However, it is an extremely polarizing topic. Disagreements will always exist when two or more people of different mindsets come together. Yeshua knew this and saw it many times in His life. So, He tells us that it is fine to disagree, but one must always remember the Golden Rule: treat people the same way you want them to treat you. The mainline denominational churches in Western Europe and Northern America are failing and this is a part of the problem. How can the church preach that they belief in Yeshua and live by His teaching of love for all while internally the people treat each other with contempt? Perhaps the consultants should stop for a minute and not tell the churches to reach out until they have cleaned up their own situations. In other words, a church should not evangelize new disciples when the church's members are not behaving like Yeshua's disciples. The church must learn to behave as it preaches. Every person in the congregation must be treated with respect and dignity, period.

Matthew 7:13-23

Language

New American Standard 1995	Koine Greek
[13] "Enter through the narrow gate; for the gate is wide and the way is broad that leads to destruction, and there are many who enter through it. [14] "For the gate is small and the way is narrow that leads to life, and there are few who find it. [15] "Beware of the false prophets, who come to you in sheep's clothing, but inwardly are ravenous wolves. [16] "You will know them by their fruits. Grapes are not gathered from thorn *bushes* nor figs from thistles, are they? [17] "So every good tree bears good fruit, but the bad tree bears bad fruit. [18] "A good tree cannot produce bad fruit, nor can a bad tree produce good fruit. [19] "Every tree that does not bear good fruit is cut down and thrown into the fire. [20] "So then, you will know them by their fruits. [21] "Not everyone who says to Me, 'Lord, Lord,' will enter the kingdom of heaven, but he who does the will of My Father who is in heaven *will enter.* [22] "Many will say to Me on that day, 'Lord, Lord, did we not prophesy in Your name, and in Your name cast out demons, and in Your name perform many miracles?' [23] "And then I will declare to them, 'I never knew you; DEPART FROM ME,	[13] Εἰσέλθετε διὰ τῆς στενῆς πύλης· ὅτι πλατεῖα ἡ πύλη, καὶ εὐρύχωρος ἡ ὁδὸς ἡ ἀπάγουσα εἰς τὴν ἀπώλειαν, καὶ πολλοί εἰσιν οἱ εἰσερχόμενοι δι' αὐτῆς· [14] τί στενὴ ἡ πύλη, καὶ τεθλιμμένη ἡ ὁδὸς ἡ ἀπάγουσα εἰς τὴν ζωήν, καὶ ὀλίγοι εἰσὶν οἱ εὑρίσκοντες αὐτήν. [15] Προσέχετε δὲ ἀπὸ τῶν ψευδοπροφητῶν, οἵτινες ἔρχονται πρὸς ὑμᾶς ἐν ἐνδύμασιν προβάτων, ἔσωθεν δέ εἰσιν λύκοι ἅρπαγες. [16] Ἀπὸ τῶν καρπῶν αὐτῶν ἐπιγνώσεσθε αὐτούς· μήτι συλλέγουσιν ἀπὸ ἀκανθῶν σταφυλήν, ἢ ἀπὸ τριβόλων σῦκα; [17] Οὕτως πᾶν δένδρον ἀγαθὸν καρποὺς καλοὺς ποιεῖ· τὸ δὲ σαπρὸν δένδρον καρποὺς πονηροὺς ποιεῖ. [18] Οὐ δύναται δένδρον ἀγαθὸν καρποὺς πονηροὺς ποιεῖν, οὐδὲ δένδρον σαπρὸν καρποὺς καλοὺς ποιεῖν. [19] Πᾶν δένδρον μὴ ποιοῦν καρπὸν καλὸν ἐκκόπτεται καὶ εἰς πῦρ βάλλεται. [20] Ἄρα γε ἀπὸ τῶν καρπῶν αὐτῶν ἐπιγνώσεσθε αὐτούς. [21] Οὐ πᾶς ὁ λέγων μοι, Κύριε, κύριε, εἰσελεύσεται εἰς τὴν βασιλείαν τῶν οὐρανῶν· ἀλλ' ὁ ποιῶν τὸ θέλημα τοῦ πατρός μου τοῦ ἐν οὐρανοῖς. [22] Πολλοὶ ἐροῦσίν μοι ἐν ἐκείνῃ τῇ ἡμέρᾳ, Κύριε, κύριε, οὐ τῷ σῷ ὀνόματι προεφητεύσαμεν, καὶ τῷ σῷ ὀνόματι δαιμόνια ἐξεβάλομεν, καὶ τῷ σῷ ὀνόματι δυνάμεις πολλὰς ἐποιήσαμεν; [23] Καὶ τότε ὁμολογήσω αὐτοῖς ὅτι Οὐδέποτε ἔγνων ὑμᾶς· ἀποχωρεῖτε ἀπ' ἐμοῦ οἱ ἐργαζόμενοι τὴν ἀνομίαν. [24] Πᾶς οὖν ὅστις ἀκούει μου τοὺς λόγους τούτους καὶ ποιεῖ αὐτούς, ὁμοιώσω αὐτὸν ἀνδρὶ φρονίμῳ, ὅστις ᾠκοδόμησεν τὴν οἰκίαν αὐτοῦ ἐπὶ τὴν πέτραν·

YOU WHO PRACTICE LAWLESSNESS.'	

Process of Discovery

Linguistics Section

Linguistic Structure

[The Narrow Gate parable] [13] "Enter through the narrow gate; for the gate is wide and the way is broad that leads to destruction, and there are many who enter through it. [14] "For the gate is small and the way is narrow that leads to life, and there are few who find it.

[False prophets] [15] "Beware of the false prophets, who come to you in sheep's clothing, but inwardly are ravenous wolves.

A [16] "You will know them by their fruits. Grapes are not gathered from thorn *bushes* nor figs from thistles, are they? [17] "So every good tree bears good fruit, but the bad tree bears bad fruit.

    B[18] "A good tree cannot produce bad fruit, nor can a bad tree produce good fruit.

A' [19] "Every tree that does not bear good fruit is cut down and thrown into the fire. [20] "So then, you will know them by their fruits.

A [21] "Not everyone who says to Me, 'Lord, Lord,' will enter the kingdom of heaven, but he who does the will of My Father who is in heaven *will enter.*

    B [22] "Many will say to Me on that day, 'Lord, Lord, did we not prophesy in Your name, and in Your name cast out demons, and in Your name perform many miracles?'

A' [23] "And then I will declare to them, 'I never knew you; DEPART FROM ME, YOU WHO PRACTICE LAWLESSNESS.'

ALTERNATE LINGUISTIC STRUCTURE

A [13] "Enter through the narrow gate; for the gate is wide and the way is broad that leads to destruction, and there are many who enter through it. [14] "For the gate is small and the way is narrow that leads to life, and there are few who find it.

B [15] "Beware of the false prophets, who come to you in sheep's clothing, but inwardly are ravenous wolves.

> **C** [16] "You will know them by their fruits. Grapes are not gathered from thorn *bushes* nor figs from thistles, are they? [17] "So every good tree bears good fruit, but the bad tree bears bad fruit. [18] "A good tree cannot produce bad fruit, nor can a bad tree produce good fruit.

B' [19] "Every tree that does not bear good fruit is cut down and thrown into the fire. [20] "So then, you will know them by their fruits.

A' [21] "Not everyone who says to Me, 'Lord, Lord,' will enter the kingdom of heaven, but he who does the will of My Father who is in heaven *will enter*. [22] "Many will say to Me on that day, 'Lord, Lord, did we not prophesy in Your name, and in Your name cast out demons, and in Your name perform many miracles?' [23] "And then I will declare to them, 'I never knew you; DEPART FROM ME, YOU WHO PRACTICE LAWLESSNESS.'

Discussion

When determining the linguistic structure of a passage it is possible to see more than one possibility. For this passage two structures are offered.

Questioning the Passage

1. How can the narrow gate be wide? (v. 13)

   Verse 13 is probably referring to two different gates. The narrow and small gate is referring to the door of a house. The door of homes where small and narrow. The gates leading into the vineyard or gardens were wider to allow animals to easily pass through.

2. What gate is being referred to that leads to destruction? (v. 13)

   The gate that leads to Hell and Satan is easy to go through because there are few requirements at this door. The metaphor is that the gate is one's behavior and attitudes during a lifetime.

3. What does the metaphor "sheep's clothing" mean? (v. 15)

    This metaphor is a reference to the false prophets who come looking and sounding like the prophets sent by the LORD. The difference between a prophet of the LORD and a false prophet is by listening to their words and viewing their actions.

4. What does the metaphor "ravenous wolves" mean? (v. 15)

    Matthew sees the false prophet as ravenous wolves being the Christian prophets of other Yeshua movements, for example the Gnostics.[72] The proto-orthodox church felt it needed to defend itself from any form of Christianity that was not theirs. The proto-orthodox church would seek out the members of the "false" movement and destroy them. The church also destroyed the writings of these movements. We know about the movements because of letters that Bishops wrote to the churches warning them about the "false" Christian movements.

5. What does the metaphor "good fruit" mean? (v. 17)

    Good fruit are good works that are done for the LORD.

6. What does the metaphor "bad fruit" mean? (v. 17)

    Bad fruits are evil works that are done for Satan.

7. What does the metaphor "cut down and thrown into the fire" mean (v. 19)?

    Productive soil is very rare in the Middle East. Therefore, a tree that cannot produce good fruit will be cut down. The tree is then used for fuel. Yeshua is connecting people who do not produce good words, thus not performing the LORD's mitzvot, should be removed from the community. The wicked will destroy a community. It

---

[72] The New Interpreter's Bible. Nashville: Abingdon Press, 2006.

is up to the community to remove the wicked because eventually their behavior will destroy it.[73]

8. Why is the word Lord repeated twice in verse twenty-one?

For the community that Matthew wrote this Gospel this is an eschatological term meaning that there will be members of the community who do not recognize the lordship of Yeshua. There are people in today's church who do not believe in the Lord Yeshua's acts of salvation. On judgment day these people will not be able to redeem themselves.[74]

It is possible that at the time of Matthew's Gospel the question of the divinity of Yeshua was being discussed. Was Yeshua divine or not? Saying Lord, Lord, would then be an acknowledgment of the divinity of Yeshua.[75]

9. What does verse twenty-two mean?

"On that day" is a reference to the day of the LORD's judgment. There will be people who did not follow the words and ways of Yeshua. Those people will find that they are shutout of Heaven. The people who followed Yeshua and followed Yeshua's' commandments will enter heaven.

10. What does it mean to "never know" a person? (v. 23)

The LORD knows a person means that He knows what one is truly feeling and thinking. Our actions and words show the LORD how much be believe in Him. On judgment day Yeshua will say that He does not know the people who rejected

---

[73] Errico, Rocco A., and George M. Lamsa. Aramaic Light on Ezekiel, Daniel, and the Minor Prophets: A Commentary Based on the Aramaic Language and Ancient Near Eastern Customs. Smyma, GA: Noohra Foundation, 2012.

[74] e, David E., David Allan. Hubbard, Glenn W. Barker, John D. W. Watts, and Ralph P. Martin. Word Biblical Commentary. Waco, TX: Word Books, 1997.

[75] Stern, David H. Jewish New Testament Commentary. Clarksville, MD: Jewish New Testament Publications, 1999.

His teaching. Those persons will not have the imputed righteousness of Yeshua upon them and will face the wrath of the LORD alone.

Verse Comparison on citations or proof text

1. [23] "And then I will declare to them, 'I never knew you; DEPART FROM ME, YOU WHO PRACTICE LAWLESSNESS.' (Matt. 7:23 NAU)

This reference is from Psalm 6:8.

[6] For the LORD knows the way of the righteous, But the way of the wicked will perish. (Ps. 1:6 NAU)

The Septuagint reads:

[8] Depart from me, all ye that work iniquity; for the Lord has heard the voice of my weeping. (Ps. 6:8 LXE)

On judgment day Yeshua will be surrounded by people who will be seeking His protection from their sins. Yeshua tells us that on judgment day those who flock to Him that are wicked will be told to leave Him. Yeshua will not save the wicked after death. During the mid-1900's Karl Barthe, a church theologian believed that everyone would have a second chance to love Yeshua and thus would be saved. This verse clearly says that is not the case. A life lived without living Yeshua's way cannot be corrected once the life is over.

Scripture cross references

Verse 15   Mar 13:22; Luk 6:26; Act 13:6; 2Pe 2:1; 1Jo 4:1; Rev 16:13; Rev 19:20; Rev 20:10; Eze 22:27; Joh 10:12; Act 20:29

Verse 16   Mat 7:20; Mat 12:33; Luk 6:44; Jam 3:12

Verse 19   Luk 3:9; Luk 13:7; Joh 15:2, Joh 15:6

Verse 23   Psalm 6:8

Culture Section

Questioning the passage

1. What is the narrow gate? (v. 13)

   The Peshitta reads "Enter in through the narrow door…" By using this translation, the following is derived. Near Eastern homes have very narrow and low doors. The churches in the Near East also have narrow and low doors. The churches have this type of doors so that one must bend down to pass through the low and narrow portal. This is to remind all who enter that they must be humble before the LORD. Bending at the waist is a sign of humility. The door leading into the Kingdom of Heaven is something to strive for and is not an easy task to pass through.

   Gates refers to the entrance into a garden or vineyard. The gate must be larger than the door to a home because animals must be able to pass through them.[76]

   If the Koine Greek and Aramaic (Peshitta) are combined the verse could be constructed as: Enter through the narrow door; for the gate is wide and the way is broad that leads to destruction. The passage is saying that the way to enter the Kingdom of Heaven is hard and requires effort, while the entrance into Hell is easy. Also, many people will enter this realm because it is easier to be bad than it is to be good.

---

[76] Errico, Rocco A., and George M. Lamsa. *Aramaic Light on Ezekiel, Daniel, and the Minor Prophets: A Commentary Based on the Aramaic Language and Ancient Near Eastern Customs.* Smyma, GA: Noohra Foundation, 2012.

Verse 14 can be used to support this idea. So, in the Greek version the narrow and small gate is the house door. A narrow and small gate would not be used in Yeshua's time. Therefore, it is referring to the door of the house. It is possible that the writer thought of the door to the house as a narrow and small gate. A door and a gate have the same function to keep things out and to let things in.

2. What is the significance of the "broad road" in verse 13?

    The broad road in Judah were popular for caravans to travel upon. The wise traveler would avoid the broad road because this route had perils. Robbers and murderers would hide on the broad roads and rob travelers, especially those who were not part of a larger group. The narrow roads were taken by wise men. The road was steep and far away from the broad main roads. Thieves could not lie in wait to murder and plunder. It was a difficult travel but a safe one.[77]

    People who took the broad gate to the broad road could be seriously hurt. Even though this path might seem the easy way it was risky. The road that leads to the LORD is not an easy path, however it is a safer path.

3. Who were false prophets in Yeshua's day? (v. 15)

    The word *nabia* is Hebrew meaning prophet. It comes from the root *nba* meaning "to bubble up, pour forth, spring forth with a flow of words under excitement of inspiration, foretell and to announce the news." Prophets were also considered the statesmen and leaders of their times. Near Eastern people believed in prophecies and were mystically inclined. There were two classes of prophets in Israel's history: the prophets of the LORD and the prophets of Baal. The false prophets of Baal always

---

[77] IBID.

tried to imitate the words of the LORD's prophets. By doing so they attempted to show their significance and power. Yeshua warns us about the false prophets that will sound legitimate but are not.[78]

4. What is the metaphor "by their fruits" mean? (v. 16-17)

In the Near East two trees of the same species may grow side by side, but the quality of the fruit can be different. One tree may produce quality fruit, while the second tree produces sour fruit. Local people know the difference and call the tree of quality fruit a good tree while the other tree is called a bad tree. Yeshua is warning us to be on the lookout for people who are false prophets. The fruit the false prophet produces must be tasted. How truthful and trustworthy is the character and deeds of the prophet? This will reveal whether this person is a good or bad prophet.[79]

Thoughts

The path to true discipleship to Yeshua is not an easy path. In Yeshua's day it meant a very difficult life and possibly no rewards in this life, but rewards in the world to come (Heaven). The disciples of Matthew's day had to be reminded that their lives might not improve here but it was still vital for them to remain true to the teachings of Yeshua for their spiritual souls' future. There was also a rash of false prophets that tried to sway Yeshua's followers. Some of the false prophets were from other forms of Christianity that rose during the first two hundred years after the Ascension. The Matthew community needed to protect itself from its members being pouched by these other movements. Did Yeshua know this was going to happen? It also begs the question as to whether the proto-orthodox church is the true faith of Yeshua or not. What if the Gnostics were correct?

---

[78] IBID.

[79] IBID.

The discussion then becomes why did the LORD let the proto-orthodox movement survive and not the Gnostics. The problem with the proto-orthodox movement was that it demanded to maintain control over Yeshua's disciples who decided to follow the Yeshua movement. This can be seen in Acts when new members were required to sell their possessions and place all monies at the feet of the Apostles. This passage has been used by the church to maintain control over its members. Thus, they put their control into Yeshua's words. A group that survived through the centuries is Saint Thomas Christianity. This form of Yeshua worship looks more messianic than catholic or orthodox. Perhaps it is the true form Christianity was supposed to take.

Reflections

A concern of the modern-day church is expressed in this passage. The thought that there are false prophets in our churches today is a scary thought. The author was naïve about the attitude and behavior of church people. Should people in the church live by the teachings of Yeshua? The Golden Rule, verse 7:12, is an example. The most unforgiving people can be found in our churches as active members. There are numerous members of churches who are there for their self-gratification rather than Yeshua's glorification. This can be seen when the "volunteer" must be praised in the weekly worship every week for his/her hard work during the week. Pastors have been forced to leave their pastorates because of people like this. They are ego centered personalities to the point that they must be followed and recognized no matter what path they decide to follow. These are the false prophets Yeshua was talking about. The intentions of a member of the church must be examined before the member is given any kind of power or responsibilities. As churches shrink in population it becomes more difficult to find people who are in the church for Yeshua's glory. The author did a survey of church members in 2004 and discovered, to his dismay, that 70% of the people in the pews had an ego centric personality. The idea that Jesus died for me is a motto of the current church. That translates into what can I get out of the church for my ego. Modernism pushed the idea of individualism and the church soaked it up. So, there are plenty of false prophets in the church who are only interested in their own glory.

Matthew 7:24-29

Language

New American Standard 1995	Koine Greek
[24] "Therefore everyone who hears these words of Mine and acts on them, may be compared to a wise man who built his house on the rock. [25] "And the rain fell, and the floods came, and the winds blew and slammed against that house; and *yet* it did not fall, for it had been founded on the rock. [26] "Everyone who hears these words of Mine and does not act on them, will be like a foolish man who built his house on the sand. [27] "The rain fell, and the floods came, and the winds blew and slammed against that house; and it fell-- and great was its fall." [28] When Jesus had finished these words, the crowds were amazed at His teaching; [29] for He was teaching them as *one* having authority, and not as their scribes.	[24] Πᾶς οὖν ὅστις ἀκούει μου τοὺς λόγους τούτους καὶ ποιεῖ αὐτούς, ὁμοιώσω αὐτὸν ἀνδρὶ φρονίμῳ, ὅστις ᾠκοδόμησεν τὴν οἰκίαν αὐτοῦ ἐπὶ τὴν πέτραν· [25] καὶ κατέβη ἡ βροχὴ καὶ ἦλθον οἱ ποταμοὶ καὶ ἔπνευσαν οἱ ἄνεμοι, καὶ προσέπεσον τῇ οἰκίᾳ ἐκείνῃ, καὶ οὐκ ἔπεσεν· τεθεμελίωτο γὰρ ἐπὶ τὴν πέτραν. [26] Καὶ πᾶς ὁ ἀκούων μου τοὺς λόγους τούτους καὶ μὴ ποιῶν αὐτούς, ὁμοιωθήσεται ἀνδρὶ μωρῷ, ὅστις ᾠκοδόμησεν τὴν οἰκίαν αὐτοῦ ἐπὶ τὴν ἄμμον· [27] καὶ κατέβη ἡ βροχὴ καὶ ἦλθον οἱ ποταμοὶ καὶ ἔπνευσαν οἱ ἄνεμοι, καὶ προσέκοψαν τῇ οἰκίᾳ ἐκείνῃ, καὶ ἔπεσεν· καὶ ἦν ἡ πτῶσις αὐτῆς μεγάλη. [28] Καὶ ἐγένετο ὅτε συνετέλεσεν ὁ Ἰησοῦς τοὺς λόγους τούτους, ἐξεπλήσσοντο οἱ ὄχλοι ἐπὶ τῇ διδαχῇ αὐτοῦ· [29] ἦν γὰρ διδάσκων αὐτοὺς ὡς ἐξουσίαν ἔχων, καὶ οὐχ ὡς οἱ γραμματεῖς.

Process of Discovery

Linguistics Section

Linguistic Structure

A [24] "Therefore everyone who hears these words of Mine and acts on them, may be compared to a wise man who built his house on the rock.

> **B** [25] "And the rain fell, and the floods came, and the winds blew and slammed against that house; and *yet* it did not fall, for it had been founded on the rock.

A' [26] "Everyone who hears these words of Mine and does not act on them, will be like a foolish man who built his house on the sand.

> **B'** [27] "The rain fell, and the floods came, and the winds blew and slammed against that house; and it fell-- and great was its fall."

[Statement] [28] When Jesus had finished these words, the crowds were amazed at His teaching;[29] for He was teaching them as *one* having authority, and not as their scribes.

Discussion

This passage is the conclusion of the Sermon on the Mount. It has an A-B-A'-B' chiasm.

Questioning the Passage

1. Who were the Scribes and how did they receive their authority?

   "The scribes make up another group of individuals who enjoyed the authority of leadership in Israel. In the New Testament they are associated with the Pharisees and the High Priests as opponents of Jesus. In the Mishnah they are presented as pre-rabbinic teachers with authority, as well as copyists and teachers. Josephus does not list them as a distinct group.

   The scribes have a notable history. All ancient peoples had large numbers of scribes for the transmission of religious texts and other legal and historical documents. In the

Old Testament the best-known scribe is Ezra; because he was both a scribe and a priest, he was a very powerful religious leader (Ez. 7:6)."[80]

Sometime before Yeshua's day a group of educated people became Scribes. A part of their work was to make copies of the Hebrew Scripture. To make the copies a man had to be very knowledgeable in the Hebrew language and the stories of the Scriptures. The Scribe who was making a copy of the Scripture had a list of rules to follows:[81]

1. They could only use clean animal skins, both to write on, and even to bind manuscripts.

2. Each column of writing could have no less than forty-eight, and no more than sixty lines.

3. The ink must be black, and of a special recipe.

4. They must verbalize each word aloud while they were writing.

5. They must wipe the pen and wash their entire bodies before writing the word "Jehovah," every time they wrote it.

6. There must be a review within thirty days, and if as many as three pages required corrections, the entire manuscript had to be redone.

7. The letters, words, and paragraphs had to be counted, and the document became invalid if two letters touched each other. The middle paragraph, word and letter must correspond to those of the original document.

8. The documents could be stored only in sacred places (synagogues, etc.).

9. As no document containing God's Word could be destroyed, they were stored, or buried, in a genizah - a Hebrew term meaning "hiding place." These were usually kept in a synagogue or sometimes in a Jewish cemetery.

---

[80] "7. The Scribes." Bible.org. Accessed October 10, 2018. https://bible.org/seriespage/7-scribes.
[81] Manning, Scott. "Process of Copying the Old Testament by Jewish Scribes." Historian on the Warpath. February 17, 2018. Accessed October 10, 2018. https://scottmanning.com/content/process-of-copying-the-old-testament-by-jewish-scribes/.

The Scribes were given authority over the Scripture since they were the copiers of it and knew it the best. During Yeshua's time the Scribes used their power to tell people how to live. This was probably happening before Yeshua. The important note is that the authority of the Scribes was given to them by the people.

It was important for the Scribes to know the authority given to any person who dared to offer an alternate view of the Scripture. Yeshua offered many alternatives. The Sermon on the Mount is the best example of Yeshua's teaching being a completely different interpretation of the Scripture.

Culture Section

Discussion

In the Near East many towns and villages were built against mountain slopes. Houses that were built on rocks could have a wall of the house hewn out of the rocky slope. With the walls being made of rock they could withstand most storms and these homes were very secure. Houses were also built near the edge of the village next to the sand. This was done because of the lack of space to build enough homes into the rocks. These homes were subject to floods that occurred during the rainy season. A dry valley could turn into a raging river during the rainy season. The homes built on sand could easily be washed away. Homes built on a rover bank could be inundated. The walls of these homes could easily collapse and crumble and eventually take down the entire house. In the rainy season the waters could reach the houses built on the rock, but the water was not strong enough to destroy these houses.

This passage is a metaphor of how people built their lives. Some people built their lives upon the foundation of truth through Yeshua's teaching. Yeshua's teaching holds firm like a rock. Some people build their lives on misleading doctrines and teaching that shift like sand. Rains, flood and wind represent evil inclination, temptation and persecutions, which are bound to come. Only the people who built their lives on the solid rock, Yeshua's' teachings, will endure.[82]

Culture and Linguistics Section

Discussion

Yeshua concludes the Sermon on the Mount with a set of statements that can only be fully understood using His culture. Therefore, a literal reading of the passages would lead the reader to potentially inaccurate conclusions. The parable offered is built on the culture of Yeshua's day. Sometimes a family was forced to build a house on the edge of town where the sand commenced. Did the community control who got to build on which piece of land? Since a son built onto His father's house, when he got married, he may be forced to build his house near or on the sand so that it connected to the original house. Smart building owners purchased as much of the mountain slops property that they could to ensure that future generations could build their homes against the rocky slopes.

Thoughts

The conclusion of the Sermon on the Mount has Yeshua telling us that those who hear His words and live by them will be living a life that will be fruitful. The best way to serve the LORD is to follow all Yeshua's words and commandments. The reader must be careful and must analyze the words that we have because of the translation of Yeshua's Words which were in Aramaic and Hebrew to Greek then to English. Along the way of translation some of the words probably changed and that could change the possible meaning of the

---

[82] Errico, Rocco A., and George M. Lamsa. *Aramaic Light on the Gospel of Matthew: A Commentary on the Teachings of Jesus from the Aramaic and Unchanged Near Eastern Customs.* Santa Fe, NM: Noohra Foundation, 2000.

message in the new language. In addition, it is well documented that people like Jerome changed parts of the Scriptures when he translated the Bible from Greek to Latin. When we consider this the question of how much of the Sermon on the Mount is Yeshua's words? It is difficult to know. However, by studying the verses using Ancient Bible Study methods the student of the Bible will get a lot closer to what is the truth. Asking questions about the Scripture is imperative to fully understand it. The interpretation of the Sermon on the Mount has been sent to us by non-Semitic people. Western/Greek people did not know how to properly read and understand Semitic story telling. The western/Greek person did not take the culture of Yeshua's day into account when reading these words. A literal reading of the Sermon on the Mount will not give the reader the proper meaning. Therefore, learn to read the Scriptures and understand them in the same way the people in Yeshua's day did.

Reflections

So, you want to live by the words of Yeshua? How do you this? The first place to start is with Yeshua's words in the Gospels. For the beginner it may be worthwhile to have said person read the Scripture literally. That is the first step of PaRDeS[83]. The second step is to read it again learning about the allegories and metaphors that are contained in the Scripture. The meaning of the passage will change as the literary structures and language barriers are discovered and become understandable. This is a way to learn about the deeper meaning of the Scripture. There are two more steps to continue the path. The next is the midrash path. Midrash writings are rare for the New Testament writings. Yeshua's words and commandments are not difficult to follow once you understand what Yeshua wanted us to know. The Scripture was written in a "code" because it was believed to have immense power. The writers did not want Gentle hands to learn the power of the Scriptures, so they

---

[83] PaRDES is an acronym for the way Scripture is analyzed by rabbis.

wove "encryption" into it. The LORD wants us to discover the code that opens the meaning of the Scripture for us. Therefore, continue searching for meaning. Ask questions about the Scripture and do not blindly accept any one's explanations.

Bibliography

n.d. *A Biblical history of Jerusalem. From Adonai to Yahweh.* Accessed October 02, 2018. http://www.bibletopics.com/biblestudy/108.htm.

n.d. *A Living Library of Jewish Texts.* Accessed July 11, 2018. https://www.sefaria.org/.

2017. *Biblical Sidon-Jezebel's Hometown.* October 20. Accessed October 02, 2018. https://www.biblicalarchaeology.org/daily/ancient-cultures/ancient-near-eastern-world/biblical-sidon-jezebel-hometown.

Davis, Anne Kimball. 2012. *The Synoptic Gospels.*

Elias, Daniel. n.d. *Tzeruf Basics.* Accessed August 16, 2018. Tzeruf Basics.

Errico, Rocco. 1997. *Setting a Trap for God: The Aramaic prayer of Jesus.* Pennsauken, NJ: BookBaby.

n.d. *Fasting and Purification.* Accessed October 11, 2018. www.greekmedicine.net/hygiene/Fasting_and_Purification.html.

Goulder, Michael Douglas. 1977. *Midrash and Lection in Matthew.* London, England: SPCK.

Hagner, Donald A. Matthew. 2015. *The WORD Commentary, Volume 33b.* Grand Rapids, MI: Zondervan.

Hoenig, Sidney B., and Avroham Yoseif, Rosenberg. 1989. *Judaica Books of the Prophets: A New Translation of the Text and Rashi.* New York, New York: Judaica Press.

Jacobs, Jill. n.d. *Jewish Attitudes Toward Poverty.* Accessed August 01, 2018. https://www.myjewishlearning.com/article/jewish-attitudes-toward-poverty/.

Jacobs, Louis. n.d. *The World to Come.* Accessed August 29, 2018. https://www.myjewishlearning.com/article/the-world-to-come/.

n.d. *Jehoshaphat, Vallye of Definition and Meaning - Bible Dictionary.* Accessed October 1, 2017. http:/www.biblestudytools.com/dictionary/jehoshaphat-valley-of/.

n.d. *Jewish Encyclopedia.* Accessed October 02, 2018. http://www.jewishencyclopedia.com/articles/13593-shittim.

2017. *Literary Structure of Gospel of Matthew.* January 31. Accessed October 11, 2018. http://www.bible.literarystructure.info/bible/40_Matthew_pericope_e.html#11.

Manning, Scott. n.d. *Process of copying the Old Testament by Jewish Scribes.* Accessed October 10, 2018. https://scottmanning.com/content/process-of-copying-the-old-testament-by-jewish-scribes/.

Mark, Joshua J. 2018. *Ancient History Encyclopedia.* October 01. Accessed October 02, 2018. http://www.ancient.eu/Tyre/.

Mayers, A.C. 1987. *The Eerdman's Bible Dictionary.* Grand Rapids, MI: Eerdmans.

n.d. *Mithras.* Accessed August 29, 2018. http://okra.stanford.edu/transcription/document_images/Vol01Scans/211_13Sept-23Nov1949_A%20Study%20of%20Mirthraism.pdf.

Mot-Kedoshim, Acharei. n.d. *The Secret of the Golden Rule.* Accessed September 26, 2018. https://kabbalah.com/en/concepts/acharei-mot-kedoshim-the-secret-of-the-golden-rule.

2018. *Mount Zion - Wikipedia.* August 29. Accessed October 02, 2018. https://en.wikipedia.org/wiki/Mount_Zion.

n.d. *Philistia - Philistines - Sea People - Crystalinks.* Accessed October 02, 2018. http://www.crystalinks.com/philistia.html.

1986. *Back to School.* Directed by Paper Clip Productions.

Scherman, Nosson. 2004. *The Prophets: the Early prophets with a commentary.* Brooklyn, NY: Mesorah Publications.

Stern, David H. 1999. *Jewish New Testament Commentary.* Clarksville, MD: Jewish New Testament Publications.

n.d. *Tag: Golden Rule*. Accessed September 26, 2018.
https://blog.hebrewseminary.org/tag/golden-rule.

2009. *Text and Interpretation Studies in the New Testament Presented to Matthew Black*. Cambridge, England: Cambridge University Press.

n.d. *The Book of the Prophet Joel*. Accessed September 28, 2018.
http://biblescripture.net/Joel.html.

1995. *The New Interpreter's Bible Commentary*. Nashville, TN: Abingdon Press.

n.d. *The Scribes*. Accessed October 10, 2018. https://bible.org/seriespage/7-scribes.

n.d. *What was the roof likely made of in Mark 2:4?* Accessed February 01, 2017.
http://hermeneutics.stackexchange.com/questions/370/what-was-the-roof-likely-made-of-in-mark-24.